LOCAL CENSUS LISTINGS

1522 - 1930

HOLDINGS IN THE BRITISH ISLES

Jeremy Gibson and Mervyn Medlycott

GW00359717

Federation of Family History Societies

First published in 1992 by the
Federation of Family History Societies.
c/o Benson Room, Birmingham & Midland Institute, Margaret Street,
Birmingham B3 3BS, U.K.

ISBN 1 872094 40 6

Cover and title page graphics by Linda Haywood.
Cover illustration: 'Presbyterian Catechising', engraving after a painting by J. Philip,
c.1830. The scene of compilation of Examination Rolls and some local censuses in
Scotland (author, Mervyn Medlycott's collection).

Typeset from computer disks prepared by Elizabeth Hampson and Jeremy Gibson.
Printed by Parchment (Oxford) Limited.

Acknowledgments

The idea of compiling this guide came from Mervyn Medlycott, who proceeded, over
the course of three years, personally to attend some 80 record offices cataloguing
material for inclusion in it. He also corresponded with librarians, archivists and the
various experts named below to bring the project to completion. However some
preliminary fieldwork in the location of census listings was made by Jeremy Gibson in
his surveys for *Census returns 1841-1881 on microfilm, Marriage, census and other
indexes,* and (aided by Christine Vialls for marriage tax assessments) for *The Hearth Tax,
other later Stuart Tax Lists and the Association Oath Rolls.* In the course of research
Jeremy Gibson also helped with the location of some additional listings. He has arranged
the guide in its present form and sub-edited the computer disk, typed by Elizabeth
Hampson, from which it has been typeset.

Archivists have as always been generous with their time assisting us when their offices
were surveyed for material and answering queries in subsequent correspondence. We
are particularly grateful to Dr. Alan Betteridge, district archivist, Calderdale Archives,
and to Roger Davey, county archivist, East Sussex Record Office, who researched their
holdings so thoroughly for us that we did not need to attend their offices in person.

We are also especially grateful to the staff of the Cambridge Group for the History of
Population and Social Structure for making accessible to us the many treasures in their
'listings files', and particularly we should like to thank Dr. Kevin Schurer and Ruth
Omoregie, librarian, for their continuing support and advice given to us.

We are most grateful to Cliff Webb, Jean Cole, Colin Chapman and Sue Wright for
sharing their knowledge and experience with us, also Gordon Johnson in Scotland and
Dr. Stephen Royle, Julian Walton and Rosemary ffolliott in Ireland, the acknowledged
experts in this field in those countries. For particular counties we are grateful for help
from Don Steel (Berkshire), Alan Dell (Buckinghamshire), Tom Sokoll (Essex), Elizabeth
Janson (Gloucestershire), Jude James (Hampshire), Bridget Lakin (Isle of Wight), Mr. R.E.
Sparry (Herefordshire), Duncan Harrington and Susan Bourne (Kent), Cliff Webb
(Middlesex and Surrey), Barbara Robinson (Warwickshire), Jean Cole (Wiltshire), Mr.
D.H. Stanley (Worcestershire), and Sylvia Mylchreest (Isle of Man).

J.S.W.G. and M.T.M.

CONTENTS

Introduction	5	Rutland	34
Further reading	10	Shropshire	34
Abbreviations	12	Somerset	35
		Staffordshire	36
England		Suffolk	37
Bedfordshire	13	Surrey	38
Berkshire	13	Sussex	39
Buckinghamshire	14	Warwickshire	40
Cambridgeshire	14	Westmorland	41
Cheshire	15	Wiltshire	41
Cornwall	16	Worcestershire	42
Cumberland	16	York and the Ainsty	43
Derbyshire	17	Yorkshire: East Riding	43
Devon	18	North Riding	44
Dorset	18	West Riding	44
Durham	19		
Essex	20	**Wales**	
Gloucestershire and Bristol	21	Anglesey	46
Hampshire	22	Caernarvonshire	46
Herefordshire	23	Cardiganshire	46
Hertfordshire	23	Carmarthenshire	46
Huntingdonshire	23	Denbighshire	46
Kent	24	Flintshire	47
Lancashire	25	Glamorgan	47
Leicestershire	26	Merioneth	47
Lincolnshire	27	Monmouthshire	47
London	28	Montgomeryshire	47
Middlesex	29		
Monmouthshire — see Wales		**Isle of Man**	48
Norfolk	30	**Channel Islands**	48
Northamptonshire	31		
Northumberland	32	**Scotland**	49
Nottinghamshire	32		
Oxfordshire	33	**Ireland**	54

INTRODUCTION

The term 'local census' was coined by population historians some twenty years ago to identify detailed inhabitants lists not connected with the 1841 to 1891 civil censuses which indicate numbers of people in each household from which the total population of a parish or township can be ascertained. By definition they must give names, at least of householders, preferably of all people and must seem to be complete for a community. Proof of completeness is however unobtainable, but then that is also true of the 1841 to 1891 civil censuses which occasionally have omitted some vagrants and gipsies.

Population enumerations which do not give names can fairly frequently be found in record offices, particularly written into parish registers. These have been excluded from this guide as they serve no useful purpose to most researchers who are looking for name lists. There is a temptation to expand the guide to include other name lists — loosely described as 'quasi- censuses' or 'census substitutes'. This we have generally resisted for two reasons. Firstly this guide is not only for use by family historians but also for social and population historians who conduct detailed analyses of whole communities and need to identify comprehensive lists from the large amount of available material of a lesser quality. Secondly this catalogue was compiled as part of the 'Gibson Guide' series, all of which chart name lists of distinct types, and it is intended to fill a particular slot in the series. Some of the other guides have produced local censuses for this; the survey for this guide has produced some new material for incorporation in the others. Seventeenth century poll taxes naming adults are certainly quasi- censuses but are catalogued in *The Hearth Tax, other later Stuart Tax Lists and the Association Oath Rolls.* Sixteenth century militia musters may name all adult males in the prime of life, but are already provided with their own guide *Tudor and Stuart Muster Rolls* and so on.

This guide has however been expanded to cover quasi- census Easter Books and Communicants Lists in England and Wales, Examination Rolls in Scotland, some lists of catholic and protestant church members in Ireland, and occasional other types, even some clearly imperfect local censuses which once were complete — types of name lists not before covered in this series. We were also fascinated enough to include the occasional drafts of 1841 to 1891 civil censuses secreted in parish and private collections, some (such as Shepshed, Leics. 1841) giving additional information not required by the Census Office — seemingly flouting the confidentiality clauses in census acts. Where there is a law, always somebody somewhere will ignore it! Now that the 100 year closure date is past, it is safe to expose these to public view.

However not all documents for census years were compiled for the government. The publicity surrounding the civil censuses encouraged private censuses to be compiled at the same time by clergy and others for their own uses, such as at Cowley, Oxfordshire, and Weston under Lizard, Staffordshire, both of 1861, whilst a 1911 census for St. Nicholas at Wade, Kent, has no connection with the civil census of that year, but was made for charity distribution of beef around the village to celebrate the coronation of King George V.

Family historians gradually became aware of the potential of local censuses to their researches in the 1960's pioneered by a study by Don Steel of Berkshire listings in 1968, and taken up by family history societies who have occasionally transcribed and indexed them, particularly in Surrey, Sussex and Warwickshire. They have been further encouraged by Colin Chapman through his talks on this subject around Britain and overseas, which he has recently (in 1990) expanded into print in his book *Pre-1841 censuses and population listings*, with a second edition in 1991.

What however was not realised by many family historians is that they were not the only people looking for local censuses. So also were population historians, encouraged by the Local Population Studies Society, and the library of the Cambridge Group for the History of Population and Social Structure was established as a depository of copies they were locating around the country. The Cambridge Group's collection now amounts to some 750 examples, many quite new to family historians. This guide is intended to bring together the fruits of investigations of historians from both disciplines to their mutual benefit.

1801 to 1831 civil censuses

Over 750 parish listings giving names have been found compiled throughout Britain for the 1801, 1811, 1821 and 1831 civil censuses. The majority are confined to naming householders with numbers in each house, sometimes divided up into males and females and in 1821 into age groupings. Some 80 name all inhabitants with a variety of other details, including relationships, occupations and ages. Only in Ireland in 1821 and 1831 were full details of all inhabitants required by the census office. In the rest of Britain compilers — overseers of the poor, teachers and clergy mostly — were not instructed to give any names at all.

Why then do so many with names survive?. The most obvious reason is that it could be very difficult, particularly in towns, to survey the population without noting some points of reference, such as householders' names, to make sure that no people were omitted or repeated. Perceiving a market, stationers, particularly in London, Essex, and Yorkshire, unofficially sold sets of printed forms for census compilation with columns requiring householders' names to be given. The statistics only were sent to the census office; the name lists, rough drafts, were put away in parish chests or found their way into private collections, from which they are now emerging. There is evidence that some of the compilers kept these drafts for other uses, particularly for poor law administration. A few have additional details added such as indicating those families in receipt of poor relief or who had gained a settlement in the parish. Some even were updated in totally new surveys in the same format for years when no national census was made, such as 1811/1815 for Middleton, Essex, 1821/1827 for St. Chad, Shrewsbury and 1821/1829 for Stowey, Somerset. Don Steel has pointed out one good reason why overseers of the poor needed detailed censuses — the Speenhamland system introduced in 1796 established that outdoor parish relief was to be provided to the poor according to the size of their families. A number of local censuses catalogued here were obviously made for poor law purposes, most notably in great detail for the town of Hungerford in 1825 and 1828, and the series of five, 1788-97 for Barham, Suffolk, mixed up with annual lists of poor inhabitants, 1784- 1843.

Other 'Official' Censuses'

In 1694 a tax was introduced, levied on births, marriages, burials, bachelors over 25 and childless widowers in England and Wales, known as the Marriage Duties Act or Marriage Tax. It was not found to be particularly successful as a source of revenue and was consequently repealed in 1705/6. Perhaps the reason was the complexity in annual documentation it required, in which two types of lists of people were to be made. The first was a census of all inhabitants of a parish or township, giving some relationships and certain income categories. Against each name was the rate of tax payable if an 'event' was to occur. The other type of list gave 'events' which had occurred upon which tax was to be paid, which very much resemble bishop's transcripts in which births, marriages and burials are recorded with names of bachelors and widowers. Copies of both types were presumably once held by the Exchequer, but have long since disappeared, victims of the remorseless weeding out process of central government departments. The only survivals have been found in borough, parish and private records in local authority record offices, of which given here are 346 of the 'census' type, most notably for the City of London of 1695. The 'bishop's transcript' type are not catalogued here, but details of them will be found in the Gibson Guide to *Hearth Taxes*, being for New Romney, Kent, 1700-6; Candleshoe wapentake, Lincs. 1701-6; Tunstead hundred, Norfolk, 1704-5; City of Oxford, 1695; Richmond, 1697-1705 and Doncaster, 1706, both in Yorkshire, and for Anglesey of 1695-1704.

'Official' censuses in another form were made in 1803 by orders of the Privy Council under the Second Defence Act, as precautions against a French invasion of Britain (detailed in the Gibson Guide to *Militia Lists and Musters*) of which some 16 are catalogued here.

Compiled on the orders of Quarter Sessions is the unique series, now published, for Westmorland of 1787. These may have been made to work out the proportion of county rate assessable on each township according to its population. A number of listings given here were located in borough records, most probably compiled for taxation or rating purposes. These include the earliest local census so far traced in Britain, naming householders with numbers in each house in Coventry in 1522.

Ecclesiastical censuses

The two largest collections to appear in this guide compiled together are for the Archdeaconry of Stafford of 1532/3 and for the Diocese of St. Asaph of the 1680s. Both were made for higher church authorities, for reasons which are none too clear, though Colin Chapman credibly suggests that the former may have been to list those 'entitled to prayers in return for some contribution to church fabric maintenance'. They do however fit into the context of great statistical surveys organised by the Church of England to chart numbers of communicants and later, nonconformists and papists in the community for whole dioceses and provinces, such as the so called '1563 census', which actually gives no names, in the Harleian Mss. at the British Library, and the Bishop Compton census of 1676, mostly statistics at the William Salt Library at Stafford. For the latter, 19 parishes have actually been found with names, catalogued here. A survey of communicants for the Diocese of Canterbury of 1565 include 40 parishes with names of which 8 enumerate the whole population. Some communicants lists in parish records were clearly the first stage in the surveying process, presumably being produced at Bishop's and Archdeacon's Visitations.

Incumbents' Visiting Books

Under this general title are all censuses compiled by parish clergy, the earliest known being for Courteenhall, Northants. of 1587. They are still being compiled today, though, for reasons of confidentiality, not catalogued here after 1930. As their name implies, the majority seem to have been made to assist the clergyman in his pastoral duties as he went round visiting his parishioners. They generally include nonconformists; some incorporate small sketch maps locating houses in the parish. Many of them display a common feature — though initially compiled at one date or within a few weeks or months, notes were added at later dates, like continuous commentaries on whole communities, sometimes over several decades. To give these in this catalogue only with compilation years would not adequately describe their scope. Therefore two dates are given — year of compilation and the year when the last information was added. One oddity included is for Inveresk, Midlothian, at which the minister took five years to get round his, admittedly large, parish, recording the inhabitants 1833-37. It is rather stretching a point to call this a census !

Obviously not all censuses made by clergy were purely or solely for house visiting purposes. Parish clergy involved themselves to a greater of lesser extent in many causes in the administration or welfare of their parishioners, requiring complete name lists to be compiled. Many played a leading role in the foundation and running of schools, charity distributions and poor relief. Some censuses in parish records note ability of people of all ages to read and write. These were most likely made either to indicate the need to set up schools or for charity distributions of bibles to households. Landowners also involved themselves in such educational causes, such as the Earl of Seaforth on the Isle of Lewis, resulting in two parish censuses compiled on his orders in 1819. Landowners also made local censuses of tenants for administration of their estates. I have only recorded those which were clearly for entire communities, most notably for the enormous estates of the Duke of Argyll, 1779 and 1792 and the Duke of Atholl, 1867-1909.

Censuses compiled by clergy can be incredibly detailed, with births, marriages, occupations, relationships, employers, literacy, schooling, even giving from personal knowledge the state of a person's health or an assessment of dependability or character. Those made at the same period as 1841 to 1891 civil censuses should not be neglected as they can fill out knowledge of people in the most unexpected ways!

Easter Books and Communicants Lists

These quasi-censuses usually record all full members of the Church of England, normally considered to be those aged over 10 or 12 in Tudor times, but somewhat older, 16 or thereabouts, later. Communicants lists were made for a variety of reasons, mostly as a record of church membership. Easter Books though were made for a specific purpose — a portion of clergy income was from receipt of tithes, and a type of small tithes were annual dues levied each Easter on full church members. It would seem possible that nonconformists were still liable to Easter dues as well as other forms of tithe, even if they did not attend the parish church; they would not however appear in communicants lists. Easter Books and Communicants Lists dated after 1800 have not been noted.

Examination or Catechismal Rolls

Inhabitants lists were compiled in Scotland of those who had been examined for their knowledge of the catechism by Church of Scotland ministers. It is not clear at what age children started to be examined, probably around 8, but the examinations were repeated even annually for people of all ages. Some fastidious ministers, or separate officials known as catechists, took the trouble to record all inhabitants in a community, even infants and free church, episcopalians and papists, and their documents are thus elevated to the category of local censuses. Communion Rolls are more common in Scottish kirk sessions records than Examination Rolls, but are not catalogued here as they do not appear to have named all adults attending the kirk, but were confined to 'the worthy' who were permitted to take communion.

Population Studies Censuses

In the eighteenth century members of the educated minority expounded at length their theories on population in learned journals such as the *Philosophical Transactions of the Royal Society*, and large numbers of population enumerations seem to have been made to support one or another argument. It would on the surface appear to be a most encouraging field to explore to try to locate local censuses, but has been, of all the types mentioned here, the most elusive and disappointing. Of those population enumerations mentioned by Colin Chapman in his recent book, only for 17 have original papers been found giving names, amongst 187 of which there seems to be no trace. Some of the enumerations were probably not compiled giving names anyway, using instead various tally systems or computed from parish registers or other sources. Of the population studies of Gregory King in the 1690s, only four local censuses made by him have been found, probably compiled from marriage tax assessments, to three of which, in Devon and Lichfield, Staffs. King added inhabitants' ages.

Those who contributed to learned journals were a minority, whilst those readers who took a passing interest in the subject may include some clergy whose local censuses survive, but who never expounded on the subject in print. Such I believe is the origin in incumbents' memoranda books of two censuses for Leverton, Lincs. of 1755 and 1762 and those at Trent, Somerset, of 1740 and 1745. Attached to the latter are notes of theories drawn from the *Philosophical Transactions* and various computations the clergyman noted on his own findings.

Some county historians before 1801 worked out parish populations for their publications, but actual name lists produced for compiling these statistics are very scarce. Only four have been found for Bedfordshire of 1788 and one each on the Isle of Wight for 1777 and Dorset for c1790.

As we have tried to make clear there were many reasons why local censuses were compiled. Among the more extraordinary were for food distribution in famine relief on the Shetland Isles in 1804, assessment of corn stocks in Clackclose hundred, Norfolk, in 1557, as evidence of the need to build a new church at Wakefield, Yorkshire, in 1723, and to establish those eligible to participate in communal celebrations at Queen Victoria's Golden Jubilee in 1887 at Wreningham, Norfolk, and Woodford, Wilts. Perhaps the oddest was at Isel, Cumberland, where the rector compiled his census in 1815 merely to decide how many new pews he needed to install in his church !

In most respects this guide follows the usual concise format of all Gibson Guides. Estimations of numbers of names have only occasionally been given for larger unindexed holdings; those for the 1801-31 civil censuses are exact numbers obtained from printed population statistics. Local censuses have been grouped into various categories, the most common of which are 'All named with ages', 'all named' and 'householders named with household numbers'. Only the latter is a barely adequate description of the largest category type, varying from those just failing to name everybody but with large amounts of other details such as ages, occupations, relationships and so on, down to tiny scraps giving householders surnames with numbers in each house. We would have liked to have expanded the categories so as for example to indicate which ones give occupations, but this would have made this arrangement much more complex and confusing. However the vast majority of documents have been personally examined in visits to over 80 record offices, so researchers can be fairly sure that all items given are as stated. Despite the scale of this survey, we believe that there are still many more local censuses to be found, and we would welcome information on those we have missed and on copies and indexes being made.

Mervyn Medlycott.

Further Reading

Mervyn Medlycott's own articles
'Local Census Listings', *Genealogists' Magazine*, vol. **23**, no. 8, pp. 281-84 (Dec. 1990).
'A Survey and Guide of Listings of Inhabitants', *Local Population Studies* jnl., no. 46, pp. 50-53 (Spring 1991).
'Pre-1841 and Local Censuses', *Greenwood Tree*, jnl. Somerset and Dorset F.H.S., vol. **15**, no. 4, pp. 131-33 (Oct. 1990).

Guides by family historians
'Earlier Censuses — Parish Censuses', by D.J.Steel, in *The National Index of Parish Registers*, vol. **1**, *Sources of Births, Marriages and Deaths before 1837*, Part I, pp. 333-36 (Society of Genealogists, 1968 and later reprints) — a pioneer survey of Berkshire listings, and still one of the best short guides.
Pre-1841 Censuses and Population Listings, by C.R.Chapman (Lochin Publishing, Dursley. 2nd edition, 1991 — a thorough survey of 18th century population enumerations, even those that do not give names, also various local censuses and quasi-censuses.

Guides by population historians
'The Study of Social Structure from Listings of Inhabitants', by P. Laslett in E.A. Wrigley (editor), *An Introduction to English Historical Demography*, pp. 160-208, also see excellent bibliography on pp. 241-263 (1966) — the pioneer and still the best introduction to this subject for historians in all fields.

also useful are:
Statistical Studies of Historical Social Structure, by K.W.Wachter and others (New York, 1978), particularly pp. 67-73
Numbering the People, by D.V. Glass (1973), particularly chapter 3.
The Development of Population Statistics, by D.V. Glass (1973).
Population in History, edited by D.V. Glass (1965).
Making Sense of the Census, by E. Higgs (H.M.S.O. 1989)
Many articles in *Local Population Studies'* jnl., nos. 1-47, also 1989 list of these articles issued by ESRC Cambridge Group and their reprint series.

Scotland
Census records for Scottish Families, by G. Johnson (Scottish Association of Family History Societies, 1990); a splendid guide to searching civil censuses and pre-1841 listings, not only for Scotland but for the whole of Britain.
Scottish Population History from the 17th century to the 1930s, edited by M. Flynn (Cambridge University Press, 1977), particularly section on 'Listings of Inhabitants' in part 2, section 4, pp. 65-69.
'Pre-1855 communion rolls and other listings in Kirk Sessions Records', by A.R. Bigwood, in *The Scottish Genealogist*, vol. **35**, no. 2 pp. 73-85 (June 1988).

Ireland
'Irish Census Returns and Census Substitutes', by R. ffolliott, which forms chapter 3 of *Irish Genealogy: A Record Finder*, edited by D.F. Begley (Heraldic Artists Ltd. Dublin, 1981 and 1987 editions); still the best catalogue to Irish name lists.
'Irish Manuscript Ecclesiastical Census Returns', by Dr. S.A. Royle, in *Local Population Studies* jnl., no. **29**, pp. 35-49 (1982).
'Irish Manuscript Census Records', by Dr S.A. Royle, in *Irish Geography*, no. **11**, pp. 110-125 (1978).

Special Subjects

1676 Compton Census: *The Compton Census of 1676; a critical edition*, by E.A. Whiteman. (Record of Social and Economic History, vol. **10**) (1986). An exhaustive study, analysing all 19 found to give names; also general background to 16th and 17th century ecclesiastical enumerations, including 1563 and 1603 censuses.

Marriage Duty Act Assessments: The introduction by D.V. Glass to *London Inhabitants within the Walls, 1695,* London Record Society, vol. **2** (1966). Detailed information on the workings of this act and survivals then located throughout England and Wales.

Easter Books and Communicants Lists: 'A Guide to Easter Books and related parish listings', by S.J. Wright, parts 1 and 2 in *Local Population Studies* jnl., nos. 42 and 43 (Spring and Autumn 1989). Examples she has cited naming all adults have been given in this guide. However she details some others giving only householders' names which we have omitted.

Abbreviations

The following abbreviations have been used, applicable throughout the guide.

AO = Archive(s) Office.

BL = British Library, Department of Manuscripts.

Bod = Bodleian Library, Oxford

CamGp = Cambridge Group for the History of Population and Social Structure. We have been requested by them to state the following:

The Library of the Cambridge Group is open weekdays during normal office   hours. The library is for reference only and is open to all; however, due to limited facilities, it is essential that readers make an appointment with the libarian prior to arrival. A photocopier is available and copies can be obtained for a small fee. All enquiries should be addressed to:

The Librarian,

Cambridge Group for the History of Population and Social Structure,

27 Trumpington Street,

Cambridge CB2 1QA.

Telephone: (0223) 333185.

GL = Guildhall Library, London.

Mf = microfilm.

Mfiche = microfiche.

Mss = manuscripts.

n.d. = no date given.

par. = parish.

PR = parish register.

PRO = Public Record Office, London.

RO = Record Office.

SoG = Society of Genealogists, 14 Charterhouse Buildings, Goswell Road, London EC1M 7BA (telephone 071 251 8799). Open to non-members, Tues. - Sat. (daily charge).

Ts = typescript.

UL = University Library. Right of access should not be assumed; please contact the Chief Librarian concerned.

BEDFORDSHIRE

Abbreviations (see also page 12)
BCL = Bedford Central Library.
BRO = Bedfordshire Record Office.
DWL = Dr. Williams's Library, Gordon Square, London.

Publications:

All named with ages: **1782-89. Cardington** [BRO P38/28/1] in David Baker, *The inhabitants of Cardington in 1782,* Bedfordshire Hist. Rec. Soc. **52** (1973); copy at CamGp.
Householders named with household numbers: **1788. Milton Ernest, Podington and Hinwick, and Thurleigh** [BL. Add. Mss. 34383 ff. 43-45] in *Bedfordshire F.H.S. jnl.,* **6** (3), 28-32 (Autumn 1987).

All named with ages
1782-89. Cardington [BRO P38/28/1], published.
1782-91. Cardington [BRO P38/28/1/2] (this is a more detailed version of the above, discovered in the church in 1977, and therefore not incorporated in printed copy above).
1911. Clapham [BRO Z 577/4].

All named
1837. Houghton Conquest (with ages of most people) [BRO P11/28/4], copy at CamGp.
1890-93. Caldecott (with birthdates of children) [BRO P142/25/1].
1915. Sutton [BRO P123/0/1].

Householders named with household numbers
1750. Bolnhurst [DWL Jones Mss. 39.B.13(34)], photocopy at BRO in CRT 130 BOL 5.
1773. Renhold [BRO PO13 pp. 68-71], photocopy at BRO in CRT 130 REN 6, copy at CamGp.
1788. Milton Ernest, Podington and Hinwick, and Thurleigh [BL Add. Mss. 34383 ff. 43-45], transcripts at BRO in CRT 130, MIL 13 and POD 16 and THU 10. Published.
1811. Kensworth [BRO P34/28/13].
1821. Bedford, par. St. Peter (in some families, all named with ages) [BCL], photocopy at BRO in 130 BED; **Blunham** [BRO P76/28/2]; **Haynes** [BRO P6/28/3].

Householders continued
1831. Bedford, par. St. Mary [BRO P81/18/1]; **Ravensden** [BRO X65/147]; **Silsoe** [BRO P54/28/21, and transcript in CRT 130 SIL 14].
1860. Stotfold [BRO P83/28/2].
1872. Eversholt [BRO P42/28/3/37].

Communicants Lists
1678-80, 1683, 1701-02. Meppershall [BRO P29/1/0 and Mf. copy].
1749-50. Bolnhurst [DWL Jones Mss. 39.B.13(36)].

BERKSHIRE

Abbreviations (see also page 12)
BRO = Berkshire Record Office.

Publications
All named: **1801. Binfield** [BRO D/P 18/18/3/1-2] in *Berkshire F.H.S. jnl.,* **3** (2-4) (1978).

Householders named with household numbers **1821. Caversham** [BRO D/P 162/18/9] in *Caversham Parish Records,* ed. J. Townsend (1989).

All named with ages
1822. Brimpton [BRO D/P 26/12/6].
1825-35, 1828-31. Hungerford (very detailed) [BRO D/P 71/28/7, 8, 8A and Mf. 150], copies at CamGp.

All named
1780-1801, 1794, 1797, 1799. Binfield [BRO D/P 18/18/2, 2A and Mf. 83], copies at CamGp.
1801. Binfield (some additions to c.1850) [BRO D/P 18/18/3/1-2 and Mf. 83], copy at CamGp. published.

Householders named with household numbers
1768, 1790, 1821. Brightwalton (1821 incomplete) [BRO D/EW 08 pp. 182-185, 188-190 and 230].
1779, 1790. Binfield [BRO D/P 18/18/1A and Mf. 83], copies at CamGp.
1782, 1788 and n.d., c.1789. Combe (n.d. c.1789 incomplete) [BRO D/P 197/1/2 and Mf. 97192] copies at CamGp.

Berkshire: *Householders continued*

1799. Buckland [BRO D/P 27/28/7].
1801, 1811. Brightwell [BRO D/P 25/18/1].
1801. Hampstead Marshall [BRO D/EX 10 pp.
38-39]; Pangbourne [BRO D/P 91/28/1 and
Mf. 197]; Tilehurst [BRO D/P 132/18/11 and
Mf. 414].
1811. Blewbury [BRO D/P 20/28/5]; Cumnor
[BRO D/P 45/18/2 and Mf. 102]; Newnham
[BRO D/P 161B/28/1].
1815. Coleshill [BRO D/P 40/28/11].
1821. Caversham [BRO D/P 162/18/9],
published; East Hendred [BRO D/P
66/28/2]; Sonning (liberty of Earley only)
[BRO D/P 113/18/2].
1831. Shellingford [BRO D/P 109/1/5 and Mf.
449].
n.d. c.1838. Milton [BRO D/P 85/28/1].
1842. Stratfield Mortimer (Mortimer Church
End only) [BRO D/EBy E135].
1854. Englefield [BRO D/EBy E142].
1859. Stratfield Mortimer [BRO D/P
120/28/7].
1868-70. Ufton Nervet [BRO D/P 135/28/2].
n.d. c.1914. Sulhamstead Abbots and
Sulhamstead Bannister [BRO D/P 124/28/2].

BUCKINGHAMSHIRE

Abbreviations (see also page 12)
BRO = Buckinghamshire Record Office.

Publications:
All named with ages: 1831 Stoke Poges [Bod
MS. TOP. Buck e.1] forthcoming, E.
McLaughlin.
*Householders named with household
numbers:* 1760 West Wycombe [BRO BAS
71/35] forthcoming, E. McLaughlin.

All named with ages
1831. Nettleden [BRO Ashridge N20/2];
Stoke Poges [Bod MS. TOP. Buck e.1], copy
at CamGp, publication imminent.
1841. Datchet (draft civil census) [BRO
PR60/32/40].
1850. Prestwood (parish created 1852) [BRO
PR168A/28/3].

All named
1696, 1702. Quainton (1696 liberty of
Shipton Lee only) [BRO PR169/28/6], copies
at CamGp.

Buckinghamshire *continued*

Householders named with household numbers
1730. Stone and Hartwell [BRO PR96/1/1],
copy at CamGp.
1749. Denham (also wives named) [BRO
D/W/86], copy at CamGp.
1749-51. Medmenham (in some families, all
people named, portrait caricatures of some
inhabitants) [BRO acc. no: AR16/89].
n.d. c.1750. Nether or Lower Winchendon
[BRO photocopy in D/X 525], copies at
CamGp and SoG.
1760. West Wycombe [BRO BAS 71/35 and
photocopy], copy at CamGp. Publication
imminent.
1787, 1811. Lathbury [BRO PR124/3/12].
1801. Beachampton [BRO PR13/28/3]; Iver
[BRO PR115/7/1 and photocopy]; Wooburn
[BRO PR240/28/10 and computer printout
copy], copy at SoG.
1811. Ravenstone [BRO PR174/3/1].
1821, 1831. Princes Risborough [BRO
PR175/28/3,4 and photocopies].
1821. Chesham (hamlets of Botley, Waterside
and Lattimers only) [BRO PR44/18/33];
Olney [BRO PR159/3/3 and photocopy].
n.d. clearly 1821. Chenies [BRO PR42/7/1];
Iver [BRO PR115/7/2].
1839. Lathbury (in some families all people
named some with ages) [BRO PR124/3/12].

Easter Books

1730, 1731. Loughton [BRO PR137/5/1].

CAMBRIDGESHIRE

Abbreviations (see also page 12)
CRO = Cambridgeshire Record Office.
CUL = Cambridge University Library.

Publications:
All named: 1843-45. Croydon [CRO
P53/1/11] in *The Rector and his flock*, ed. D.
Ellison (1980).

All named with birth/baptism dates
1874. Barrington [CRO P8/7/1].

Cambridgeshire *continued*

All named

1686. Great Abington [CRO 619/21], copy at CamGp.

1802. Hinxton [CUL Add. Mss. 5821], copy at CamGp.

1843-45. Croydon [CRO P53/1/11], copy at CamGp., published.

1895-99. March par. **St. John** [held by incumbent, Station Road, March].

1910. Hardwick [CRO P83/3/1].

Householders named with household numbers

1749, 1815, 1821. Cambridge par. **St. Benedict** [CRO P25/18/30, 31 and P25/28/1, 2,3], copies at CamGp.

n.d. c.1760. Cambridge par. **St. Giles** and **Cambridge,** par. **St. Peter** [Bod. Gough, Cambs. 76].

1781. Landbeach [CRO photocopy in R91/9], copy at CamGp.

1786, 1811. Trumpington [CRO P158/3/2, 4].

1798. Gamlingay [CRO P76/7/2], copy at CamGp; **Landbeach** [CRO P104/1/4], copy at CamGp.

1801, 1811, 1821. Cambridge par. **St. Edward** [CRO P28/18/17, 18, 19].

1801, 1811. Cambridge par. **St. Mary the Great** [CRO P30/18/8, 9].

1801. Ely par. **St. Mary** [CRO P68/18/4]; **Girton** [CRO P77/1/2]; **Little Wilbraham** [CRO P175/25/1].

1810. Hildersham [CRO P91/28/3].

1811. Balsham [CRO P7/18/4]; **Ely** par. **St. Mary** [CRO R81/36].

1821. Downham [CRO P57/19/14]; **Duxford** [CRO photocopy in R91/9], copy at CamGp.

1831. Melbourn [CRO photocopy in R91/35], copy at CamGp.

n.d. c.1838 Trumpington [CRO P158/16/10].

1854. Swaffham Bulbeck [CRO P149/28/2], copy at CamGp.

1860. Kirtling (with householders ages) [CRO P101/28/8].

1888, 1889, 1891, 1900, 1910. Tadlow [CRO P152/1/3].

1910. East Hatley [CRO P152/1/3].

CHESHIRE

Abbreviations (see also page 12)

CCRO = Chester City Record Office.
CRO = Cheshire Record Office, Chester.
SRO = Shropshire Record Office, Shrewsbury.

Publications:

Index to surnames in 1821 census of Rosthern (see below) in *F.H.S. of Cheshire jnl.*, 1 (2-4, March to Sept. 1970).

All named with ages

1811, 1821, 1831. Alderley [CRO P143/13/15, 16, 17], copies at CamGp.

1821. Rosthern (High Legh, Millington, Over Tabley, Tatton, and parts of Agden and Bollington townships only) [CRO P47/10/6], index published.

All named

1831-33, 1831-34, 1839. Warburton (two versions for 1831, one for civil census, other an incumbent's visiting book) [CRO P68/19/3, 4 and P68/10/1], copies at CamGp.

All adults named

1641. Chester, Eastgate ward [CCRO Cas. 1, ff. 2, 234-9]; **Chester,** St. Giles ward [CCRO Cas. 1, ff. 6]; **Chester,** par. **St. John** (incomplete) [CCRO Cas. 1, ff. 9].

Householders named with household numbers

1645/6. Chester (whole city within the walls (2,000), compiled during civil war siege of Chester) [BL Harleian Mss. 2135. Mf. copy at CCRO], copy at CamGp.

1801. Marbury [SRO 3091/X/1 ff. 237].

1827. Church Hulme (chapelry in par. Sandbach) [CRO P82/14/3].

1831. Stockport (Handforth township only) [CRO P10/18/19]; **Tattenhall** (Tattenhall township only) [CRO P5/26/3].

1838-56. Bebington [CRO P62/15/7].

1848-78. Davenham [CRO P6/16/28].

1865. Middlewich (Byley cum Yatehouse township only) [CRO P100/15/2].

Easter Books

1587, 1598, 1612, 1620, 1642, 1644, 1670-76. Chester, par. **St. John** [CCRO BN 39, 40].

1767. Brereton [CRO D/Acc. 175/8].

1799-1826. Eastham [CRO DDX 378/36].

CORNWALL

Abbreviations (see also page 12)
CRO = Cornwall Record Office, Truro.

Publications:
Easter Books: **1588-96. St. Just in Penwith**
[location not known] in jnl. *Royal Institute
of Cornwall*, 20, 213-94, ed. J. Taylor (1918).

Householders named with household numbers
1801. St Hilary [CRO P87/1/4].
1811. Poundstock [CRO P193/5/1].
1821. Boyton [CRO P16/16b/2/1]; **Veryan**
[CRO P244/16b/1].
n.d. **c.1824. St Breock** [CRO P19/28/14].
n.d. **c.1841. Poundstock** (appears to have
been compiled same time as 1841 civil
census, but giving quite different
information) [CRO P193/2/1/1/], copy at
CamGp.

CUMBERLAND

Abbreviations (see also page 12)
CRO = Cumbria Record Office, Carlisle.

Householders named with household numbers
1685. Whitehaven [CRO D/LONS/W1/33 pp.
6-7], copy at CamGp.
1762. Whitehaven [CRO D/LONS/W and Ts.
copy in search room], copies at CamGp and
SoG.
1765. Maryport [CRO D/Ben/3481], copies at
CamGp and SoG.
1792. Maryport [CRO Ts. copy from original
in private hands in D/CR/12], copies at
CamGp and SoG.
1811, 1815. Isel [CRO PR/141/32/2].
1821. Holm Cultram [CRO PR/122/42];
Newton Reigny (Newton Reigny and
Catterlen townships only) [CRO PR/6/21];
Skelton (Skelton, Lamonby and Unthank
townships only) [CRO PR/10/192-4].
1925. Great Salkeld [CRO PR/116/69].

DERBYSHIRE

Abbreviations (see also page 12)
DRO = Derbyshire Record Office, Matlock.
SA = Sheffield Archives.

Publications:
All named with children's ages: **1811.**
Littleover [DRO D2728A/P1 1/2d] in
printed parish register of Littleover. Copy at
CamGp.
All named with children's ages: **1811.**
Mickleover [DRO D2728A/P1 1/2c] in
printed parish register of Mickleover. Copy
at CamGp.
All named; **1695. Melbourne** [original not
found] in *jnl. Derbyshire Arch. and Nat.
Hist. Soc.,* 7, 1-30 (1885), indexed. Copy at
CamGp.

All named with ages
1821. Mackworth [DRO D1052A/PO 13].
1831. Whittington (very detailed) [DRO
D3356/1 and photocopy in D3356/2].

All named with children's ages
1811. Mickleover [DRO D2728A/PI 1/2c and
Mf. copy XMI/269/3], published; **Findern**
(chapelry in par. Mickleover) [DRO
D862A/PI 1/2]; **Littleover** (chapelry in par.
Mickleover) [DRO D2728A/PI 1/2d and Mf.
copy XMI/269/3], published.
n.d. **c.1849. Pinxton** [DRO D740A/PI 6/1].

All named
1695. Melbourne, see publications.
1696. Darley [SA Bar D. 728], copy at
CamGp.
1696, 1698. Tibshelf [DRO D1091A/PO 2].
1774. Morley (incomplete) [DRO D1797A/PI
1/2 and Mf. copy XMI/303/2]
n.d. **c.1830. Smisby** (mostly with ages) [DRO
D2375M/41/6].
1843. Alvaston [DRO D878A/PI 54].

Householders named with household numbers
1787, 1801, 1811. Morley [DRO D1797A/PI
1/2, 3 and Mf. copies XMI/303/2, 3], copies
of 1787, 1801 at CamGp.
1792. Barlborough [DRO photocopy of lost
original in D3481/1/1], copies at CamGp
and SoG.
1801, 1821. Eckington [DRO D750A/PO 200,
204].
1801. Clowne [DRO D1296A/PI 1/3 and Mf.
copy XMI/49/9]; **Smalley** [DRO D784A/PI
1/7 and D784A/PO 1/1 and Mf. copy
XMI/334/10], copies at CamGp and SoG.

Householders continued
1811, 1821. Crich (1821 incomplete) [DRO
D2365A/PO] (both at present unfit for
production).
1811. Hope [DRO D1038A/PO 223, 224].
1814. Hathersage [DRO D1970A/'census'].
1821. Chesterfield (Newbold and Dunston
township only) [DRO D2262Z/PO 98];
Doveridge [DRO D1197A/PO 1857 and Mf.
copy XMI/325/1]; **Mickleover** [DRO
D2728A/PI 1/2e and Mf. copy XMI/269/3];
Ockbrook [DRO D2000A/PO 14/1];
Ticknall (incomplete) [DRO D1396A/PO
33/1].
1897, 1898. Dale Abbey [DRO D1061A/PW
3/2].
1913. Lullington [DRO D811A/PZ 6].
n.d. **c.1924. Duffield** [DRO D2402A/PI 26/1,
2].

Easter Books
n.d. **c.1600. Boylestone** [DRO D1174A/PI 23].
1671-1746. Marston on Dove [DRO
D813A/PI 392].
1701. Breadsall [DRO D2459A/PI 10/9, 10].
1710-51. Doveridge [DRO D1197A/PI 78].
1725, 1740-42, 1754-1812. Bakewell [DRO
D2057A/PI 32/1-6].
1729. Hathersage [DRO D1970A/].

DEVON

Abbreviations (see also page 12)
DRO = Devon Record Office, Exeter.
NDRO = North Devon Area Record Office,
Barnstaple.

All named with ages
1698 Buckfastleigh and **Ringmore** [BL
Harleian Mss. 6832 ff. 132-34 and 146-47],
copies at CamGp.
1779. Wembworthy [DRO 1165Z/Z 1], copy
at CamGp.
1803. Exeter, par. **St. Paul** [DRO ECA
Miscellaneous Papers Box 5]; **North Tawton**
[DRO 2914A/PM 94-106], copy at CamGp.
1821. Clyst St. George [DRO 3147A/PZ 13].
1829. Sidbury [DRO 2096A/PZ 1].

All named
1696. Sowton (incomplete) [DRO 780A/PZ
1-6].
1790, 1793, 1800. Sandford [DRO Sandford
Par. Records PX2], copies at CamGp.
1801. Bickleigh [DRO 2167A/PZ 1].
1803. Barnstaple [NDRO 3054A/PC1];
Exeter, par **St. Mary Steps** [DRO ECA
Miscellaneous Papers Box 5].
1811. Doddiscombsleigh [DRO 538A/PZ 2].
1881-88. East Down [NDRO 2006A/PR 5].
1889-1910. Uplowman [DRO 829A/PI 52].
1895-1909. Mamhead [DRO 461A add/PI 1].
1898-1907. Combe Raleigh [DRO 567A
add/PI 53].

Householders named with household numbers
n.d. **c.1700. Ottery St. Mary** [DRO 3327A
add/PZ 4]
1775, 1783. Sandford [DRO Sandford Par.
Records PX2], copies at CamGp.
n.d. **c.1801 or 1811. Mortehoe** [NDRO
3834A/PZ 1].
1821. Axminster [DRO R7/2/Z/47-49];
Dean Prior [DRO Dean Prior PF/PX9-11];
Exeter, par. **Holy Trinity** [DRO 1718A/PZ 1];
Rewe [DRO 1255A/PO 299].
n.d. clearly **1821. Bickleigh** [DRO 2167A/PZ
2].
1826-27 Uplyme [DRO 3030A add and add
2/PI 5].
1860. Huntsham [DRO 1131A/PO 5].
1864. Halberton [DRO 4074A/PZ 3].

All adult men named
n.d. **c.1750. Tavistock** [DRO
L1258M/SS/P1/14].

DORSET

Abbreviations (see also page 12)
DRO = Dorset Record Office, Dorchester.
PCL = Poole Central Library.
PTH = Town Clerk's Office, Poole Town Hall.

Publications
All named with ages: n.d. **c.1790. Corfe
Castle** (very detailed) in *History and
Antiquities of Dorset.*, J. Hutchins (2nd. edn.
1796-1815). Index in *jnl. Dorset F.H.S.* **3** (1:
Dec. 1989). Copies at DRO (photocopy 313)
and CamGp.
All named: **1724-29, 1769. Puddletown**
[DRO PE/PUD/IN 7] in Dorset Rec. Soc. **11**
(1988).
All named: **1801. Oborne** [DRO PE/OBN/RE
1] in *Somerset and Dorset Notes and
Queries,* 15, 101-104 (1916-17).

All named with ages
n.d. **c.1790. Corfe Castle**, see publications.
1821, 1831. Corfe Castle [DRO D/MOW/Z.6
and photocopy 801/2,3], copies at CamGp.
1821. Thornford [DRO PC/TFD/5/18], copy at
CamGp.

All named
1577. Lyme Regis (? householders and adult
men named only) [DRO DC/LR/N6], copy at
CamGp.
**1695, 1697, 1699, 1701, 1702, 1703. Lyme
Regis** (also Colway tithing 1695 only) [DRO
DC/LR/H2], copies at CamGp.
1724-29, 1769. Puddletown [DRO
PE/PUD/IN 7], copy at CamGp published.
1800. Melbury Osmond [DRO D136/Z 1],
copy at CamGp.
1801. Oborne [DRO PE/OBN/RE 1 and
transcript in PE/OBN/IN 8], copy at CamGp
published; **Sturminster Newton** [DRO
PE/SN/OV 1, 2], copy at CamGp.
1803. Rowbarrow Hd. [DRO D286/5 and
Photocopy 747] (3,023).
1811. Corfe Castle [DRO D/MOW/Z 6 and
Photocopy 801/1], copy at CamGp.
1821. Horton [DRO PE/HOR/OV 1], copy at
CamGp; **Woodlands** [DRO PE/HOR/MI 3]
copy at CamGp.
1844-45. Bishops Caundle [DRO PE/BCD/IN
1].
1892-98. Powerstock and **West Milton** [DRO
PE/POW/IN 9/2].
1898-1907. Purse Caundle [DRO PE/PCD/IN
8].

Dorset continued

Householders named with household numbers
1574. Poole [PTH] copies at DRO (photocopy 222), PCL and CamGp.
1775. Beaminster [DRO PE/BE/MI 3/1], copy at CamGp.
1776, 1791, 1795, 1804. Tolpuddle [DRO PE/TOL/IN 3/2].
1801. Martinstown (Winterborne St. Martin) [DRO D542/1], copy at CamGp.
1803. Corfe Castle Borough [DRO PE/COC/MI 33], copy at CamGp.; **Poole Borough** [PTH] (1,389).
1811. Whitchurch Canonicorum (incomplete) [DRO PE/WCC/OV 86].
1821. Compton Abbas [DRO PE/COA/OV 2], copy at CamGp. **Litton Cheney** [DRO PE/LIC/OV 21]; **Marnhull** [DRO PE/MAL/OV 5], copy at CamGp. **Shaftesbury, par. St. James** [DRO PE/SY(SJ)/OV 1], copy at CamGp.; **Winterborne Whitechurch** [DRO PE/WWH/OV 1 and Ts. copy in search room], copy at CamGp. (original at present unfit for production).
1822. Wimborne St. Giles [DRO PE/WSG/OV 15].
1831. Allington [DRO PE/ALL/OV 4/1]; **Ryme Intrinseca** [DRO PE/RYN/IN 1].
n.d. c.1850. Winterborne Clenston and **Whatcombe** [DRO D/TRD/E 6].
1860. Longbredy and **Kingston Russell** [DRO PE/LBY/IN 20].
1903-04. Kimmeridge [DRO PE/KIG/CW 1].

co. DURHAM

Abbreviations (see also page 12)
CAM = Cleveland County Archives Department, Middlesbrough.
DRO = Durham County Record Office, Durham.
NYRO= North Yorkshire County Record Office, Northallerton.

Householders named with household numbers
1767. Darlington [NYRO ZDG(A) IV 7/1 and Mf. copy MIC 1310, frame 757], copy at CamGp.
1814. Egglescliffe [DRO EP/Eg/22. Mf. copy at CAM].
1821. Durham, par, St. Oswald (Elvet township only) [DRO EP/Du SO/111/2].
1835. Whickham [DRO EP/Whm/29].
1888-90. Eldon [DRO EP/EL/11].

Easter Books
1593-1615. Ryton [DRO EP/Ryt/1/10-12].

ESSEX

Abbreviations (see also page 12)
CRO = Essex Record Office, Colchester and N.E. Essex Branch.
ERO = Essex Record Office, Chelmsford.
GCL = Grays Central Library.
SRO = Essex Record Office, Southend Branch.
SWTH = Town Clerk's Office, Saffron Walden Town Hall.
VHM = Vestry House Museum, Walthamstow.

All named with ages
1796. Ardleigh [CRO D/P 263/1/5 and Mf. copy in T/B 216/2], copy at CamGp.
1821. Braintree [ERO D/DU 65/83] (2,983), copy at CamGp.
1831. Ingatestone [ERO D/DU 407/1], copy at CamGp.
1879-91, 1883-87. Foxearth [ERO D/P 368/28/2, 3].

All named
1695, 1697, 1699. Little Parndon [ERO D/P 34/1/2], copy of 1695 at CamGp.
1775, 1778. Terling (with children's ages) [ERO T/P 87 and copies in D/DRa E16], copies at CamGp.
1798. Woodford [ERO D/P 167/18/2], copy at CamGp.
1831. Finchingfield [ERO D/P 14/18/16], copy at CamGp; Steeple Bumpstead [ERO D/P 21/18/27], copy at CamGp; Tilbury juxta Clare [ERO D/P 164/18/17].
1887-1913. Great Leighs (some ages given) [Bod MS. TOP. Essex e42].

Householders named with household numbers
1745. Wanstead [ERO D/P 292/12/4], copy at CamGp.
1793, 1807. Bocking [ERO D/P 268/18/1, 2], copies at CamGp.
1797. Harlow [ERO D/P 32/28/2], copy at CamGp.
1801, 1810, 1831. Ashdon [ERO D/P 18/18/4, 5, 6].
1801, 1821, 1831. Little Baddow [ERO D/P 35/18/2, 3 and 35/11/2].
1801, 1821. Debden [ERO D/P 242/18/3, 5], copies at CamGp.
1801, 1811. Rainham [ERO D/P 202/18/17].
1801, 1809, 1811. Terling [ERO D/P 299/12/4, 5], copy of 1809 at CamGp.
1801, 1811. Toppesfield [ERO D/P 163/1/3 and 163/18/1 and Ts. copies in T/R 143 and Mf. copies].
1803, 1811. Rochford [SRO D/P 129/17/3 and 129/18/12. Mf. copy of 1803 at ERO].

Householders continued
1809. Wakes Colne [CRO D/P 88/18/9], copy at CamGp.
1811, 1821. Ardleigh [CRO D/P 263/28/1], copies at CamGp.
1811, 1831. Brightlingsea [CRO D/DE I 04 and D/P 312/18/2, 3].
1811, 1821. Colchester, par. St. Leonard at the Hythe [CRO D/P 245/18/18, 19].
1811,1821. Horndon on the Hill [ERO D/P 56/18/1, 2], copies at GCL and CamGp.
1811, 1821, 1831. Leyton [VHM L31. 1/1, 2, 3 and Mf. copies and indexes].
1811, 1815. Middleton [ERO D/P 394/18].
1811, 1831. Mundon [ERO D/P 238/18/6], copies at CamGp.
1811, 1821. Tilbury juxta Clare [ERO D/P 164/18/17].
1811, 1821, 1831. Walthamstow [VHM W31. 1/1, 2, 3 and Mf. copies and indexes].
1811, 1821, 1831. Woodham Walter [ERO D/P 101/18/2, 3, 4].
1811. Bradwell juxta Mare [ERO D/P 51/18/5]; Great Clacton [CRO D/P 179/18/10]; Elmstead [CRO D/P 168/18/8]; Hatfield Broad Oak [ERO D/P 4/18/2]; Great Parndon [ERO D/P 184/18/9]; St. Lawrence [ERO D/P 361/18/1]; Saffron Walden [SWTH] (669); Sandon [ERO D/P 253/18/5]; Thorrington [CRO D/P 293/18]; Wickford [ERO D/P 70/18/1]; Witham [ERO D/P 30/18/6].
1821. Beaumont cum Moze [CRO D/P 285/18/2]; Finchingfield [ERO D/P 14/18/15], copy at CamGp; Mistley [CRO D/P 343/18], copy at CamGp; Wanstead [ERO D/P 292/18/5]; Writtle [ERO D/P 50/18/10].
1827. Halstead (some ages given) [ERO D/P 96/18/6], copy at CamGp.
1829. Great Leighs [ERO D/P 137/7], copy at CamGp.
1830. Kelvedon [ERO Ts. copy of original in private hands in T/P 116/68].
1831. Little Bentley [CRO D/P 359/18/1]; Upminster [ERO D/P 117/18/6]; Wormingford [CRO D/P 185/18/13].
1839. Colchester, par. St. James [CRO D/P 138/1/1], copy at CamGp.
1840. Witham [ERO D/P 30/1/2A and 30/28/5].
1842. Coggeshall [ERO D/P 36/11/181].
1874. Terling [ERO Mf. copy of original in private hands in T/B 389/4].
1914. Great Oakley [CRO D/P 47/28/6].

GLOUCESTERSHIRE and BRISTOL

Abbreviations (see also page 12)
BCRL = Bristol Central Reference Library.
BRO = Bristol Record Office.
GCL = Gloucester Central Library.
GRO = Gloucestershire Record Office, Gloucester.

Publications
All named: 1696. Bristol all 18 parishes [BRO] in *The Inhabitants of Bristol in 1696*, edited by E. Ralph and N. Williams, Bristol Rec. Soc., 25 (1968), indexed (12,800 names).
Householders named with household numbers: 1742. Olveston [BRO P/OV/1/4] in *Bristol and Avon F.H.S journal*, 15, 18-22 (1979).
Easter Books: 1568-84. Bristol par. St. Ewen [unknown location] in *The Church Book of St. Ewens, 1454-1584.* Bristol and Gloucestershire Arch. Soc. Publications, 6, 206-45 (1967).

All named with ages
1839-65. Huntley (birthdates also given) [GRO P184/IN4/1].
1841. Painswick (original householder returns for civil census) [GRO P244/MI 10].

All named
1676. Daglingworth [GRO P107/CW 2/1], copy at CamGp.
1695-1706. Bristol [BRO marriage duties act assessments], parishes as follows: **All Saints** 1696, 97, 98, 1702, 04; **Castle Precincts** 1696, 98, 99, 1704 and two n.d.; **Christchurch** 1696, 97, 98, 99; **St. Augustine** 1696, 1704 and two n.d.; **St. Ewen** 1702 and one n.d.; **St. James** 1695, 96, 97, 99 1702, 04 and one n.d.; **St. John Baptist** 1696, 97, 98, 1704 and one n.d.; **St. Leonard** 1697, 1704 and two n.d.; **St. Mary Port** 1696, 98, 1702, 04; **St. Mary Redcliffe** 1696, 97, 99, 1702 and two for 1704; **St. Michael** 1697, 98?, 1704 and two n.d.; **St. Nicholas** 1695, 96, 97 and one n.d.; **St. Peter** 1698, 1704? and two n.d.; **SS. Philip and Jacob** 1695, 96, 98, 99, 1702, 04 and one n.d.; **St. Stephen** 1696, 98, 1702, 04; **St. Thomas** 1695, 96, 99, 1704 and one n.d.; **St. Werburgh** 1696, 97, 1702 and **Temple** 1696, 98, 99, 1704 and two for 1706. All parishes for **1696** published.
1695. Stinchcombe [GRO P312/MI 3], copy at CamGp.

All named *continued*
1696. North Nibley [GCL Smyth of Nibley Papers, vol. 4], copy at CamGp.
n.d. c.1800, 1828. Woolaston [GRO P376/IN 4/6, 7].
1806. Bibury (Ablington and Arlington townships only) [GRO D269B/F69], copy at CamGp.
1819-28. Barnsley [GRO D269B/B14], copy at CamGp.
1881-90, n.d. c.1926. Bromsberrow [GRO P63/IN 1/9, 10].
n.d. c.1888-95. Dymock (with birthdates) [GRO P125/IN 4/3].

All over age 16 named
1637-38. Bristol, par. St. James [BCRL B4531 and photocopies 30668-69].

Householders named with household numbers
1662. Abinghall, Hewelsfield, Littledean and St. Briavels [PRO F16/28], copies at CamGp.
1676. Cam and Stinchcombe [in Cam parish church, in vestry book, 1625-1730] (analysed in *The Compton Census of 1676* by E. A. Whiteman (1986)).
1735/6. Tetbury [GRO D566/Z 11], copy at CamGp.
1742. Olveston [BRO P/OV/1/4; copy at GRO photocopy 824], published.
1752. Forthampton and Swinley (manor of) [GRO D1137/1], copy at CamGp.
1781. Bristol, par. SS. Philip and Jacob (incomplete) [BCRL 21769 and photocopy 33284].
1795. Chipping Sodbury [GRO D2071/E50], copy at CamGp.
n.d. c.1800. Olveston [BRO P/OV/X/9].
1801, 1811, 1821. Great Badminton [GRO P32a/OV 9/1].
1801. Hawkesbury [GRO P170/OV 7/4].
n.d. c.1806. Bibury (Bibury township only) [GRO D269B/F90], copy at CamGp.
1811, 1821. Mickleton [GRO P216/IN 4/1].
1811. Horsley [GRO P181/OV 7/1]; **Naunton** [GRO P224/CW 4/1]; **Rendcombe** [GRO P267/OV 7].
1821, 1831. Bisley [GRO P47a/MI 1,2 and Ts. copies in PA47/16].
1821. Aust (chapelry in par. Henbury) [GRO D5944/2]; **Stratton** [GRO loose paper in P319/IN 1/7]; **Stroud**, par. St. Lawrence (whole parish except Pakenhill tithing) [GRO P320a/VE 1/1-3]; **Woolaston** [GRO P376/MI 1].

Gloucestershire: *Householders continued*

1824. Barnsley [GRO D269B/B14], copy at CamGp.
1828. Dyrham [GRO D1799/R 19].
1830, 1853. Arlingham [GRO D2685/20], copies at CamGp.
1842. Brookthorpe [GRO P64/MI 2].
1892-95. Gloucester, par. St. James [GRO P154/8 IN 1/32].

Easter Books
1568-84. Bristol, par. St Ewen, see publications.
1594-1636. Mickleton [GRO P216/IN 3/23].
1628, n.d. c.1628. Stanton [GRO P307/IN3/1].

HAMPSHIRE

Abbreviations (see also page 12)
GMR = Guildford Muniment Room, Surrey Record Office.
HL = Huntington Library, California, U.S.A.
HRO = Hampshire Record Office, Winchester.
IWRO = Isle of Wight Record Office, Newport.
RHM = Red House Museum, Christchurch (now in Dorset).
SRO = Southampton City Record Office.

Publications
All named: **1817-18. Boldre and Brockenhurst** (very detailed, many birth/baptism dates) [RHM] in *Comyn's New Forest*, ed. J.F. James (1982), with maps and index.

All named with ages
1803. Calbourne [IWRO CAL/PR/14 (old no: CAL/APR/332/1)].
1821. Winchester, par. St. Bartholomew Hyde [HRO 13M85W/160] (730).
1845. Old Alresford [HRO 43M74A/PZ 2].

All named
1695. Southampton, pars. All Saints Infra, All Saints Extra, St. Lawrence and St. Mary [SRO SC/14/2/62-65 with indexes], copies at CamGp.

Hampshire: *All named continued*

1696, 1697. Southampton, pars. All Saints Infra, All Saints Extra, Holy Rood, Portswood, St. John, St. Lawrence, St. Mary and St. Michael (whole city) [SRO SC/14/2/66-82 with indexes], copies at CamGp.
1765. Avington (with children's ages) [HL Stowe Colln. Ms. STB 149; transcript at HRO Photocopy 567], copy at CamGp.
1817-18. Boldre and Brockenhurst [RHM], see publications.
1821. East Tisted [HRO 30M82/PZ 2].
1846. Old Basing [HRO 11/M49/225].
1887. Privett [HRO 84M88/1].
1902-25. Hawkley [HRO 35M73A/PI 8].

Householders named with household numbers
1749, n.d. c.1750. Martyr Worthy [HRO 78M82/PI 6, 7 and Photocopy 84/25].
1777. Arreton [IWRO JER/WA/39/5 and Ts. copy].
1792. Old Alresford [HRO 43M74A/PZ 1], copy at CamGp.
1801, 1811, 1821, 1831. Fordingbridge [HRO 24M82/PO 20].
1801, 1811. Lymington [HRO 42M75/PZ 10a, b].
1801. Exton [HRO P86M71/PR 3], copy at CamGp; **Herriard** [HRO 44M69/J 9/79].
1811, 1821, 1831. Fawley [HRO 25M60/PO 80].
1811. Calbourne [IWRO CAL/PR/4 (old no: CAL/APR/1A/1)]; **Kings Worthy** [HRO 19M78A/PO 2].
n.d. c.1820-30. Headley [GMR PSH/HED/24/1].
1821. Newchurch (town of Ryde only) [IWRO copy of original in private hands in RYD/68], copy and index at SoG (see article on this census in *Genealogists' Magazine*, 23 (3), 103-4 (Sep. 1989)); **Wherwell** [HRO 13M67/PO 2]; **Winchester,** par. St. Peter Cheesehill or Chesil (incomplete) [HRO 3M82W/PO 7].
1828. Cliddesden [HRO 31M82/PR 4].
1831. Baughurst [HRO 58M80A/PO 18].
1854. Ringwood [HRO 22M84/PW 46].
1877. Winchester, par. St. Bartholomew Hyde (also lodgers named) [HRO 55M81W/PI 32].
1897. Bullington [HRO 61M70/PI 6].
n.d. c.1900. Lockerley and **East Tytherley** [HRO 54M71/398].

HEREFORDSHIRE

Abbreviations (see also page 12)
HRO = Hereford and Worcester Record
Office, Hereford.

All named
1781. Tarrington [HRO M27/4].
1828, 1838. Much Marcle (with children's
ages) [HRO AG56/22, 23].

Householders named with household numbers
1674. Stoke Edith [HRO E12/F/P11], copy at
CamGp.
**1676. Burghill, West Hide, Stretton Sugwas
and Sutton St. Nicholas** [HRO HD
'Compton Census'], copies at CamGp.
1799. Byford [HRO W99/3 (note this is not on
Mf. copy of this PR book)].
1801. Stoke Edith [HRO AE55/2 and Mf. copy
MX141].
1811. Lucton [HRO AC80/3 (note this is not
on Mf. copy of this PR book)].
**n.d. c.1825. Aston, Burrington, Downton,
Elton, Leinthall Starkes with Leintwardine**
(part of parish) [HRO T74/505].
1831. Mordiford [HRO AW12/13], copy at
SoG.

Easter Books
1596-1607. Ledbury [HRO A61].

HERTFORDSHIRE

Abbreviations (see also page 12)
HRO = Hertfordshire Record Office.

All named
1801, 1803. Barkway and Reed (1801 omits
servants' names) [HRO D/P 13 3/4 and 13
29/4], copies at CamGp.
1821. Digswell [HRO D/P 34 29/3], copy at
CamGp.
1892, n.d. c.1900. Aldenham [HRO D/P 3
1/15, 16].

Householders named with household numbers
1700, 1714, 1718. Kimpton [HRO D/P 61
1/1], copies at CamGp.
1764-70, 1769-70. Northchurch (some ages
given) [HRO D/P 74 3/3].
1801, 1807. Hitchin [HRO 67578, 67580],
copies at CamGp.
1803-1807 (every year) **Therfield** [HRO D/P
107 29/9], copies at CamGp.
1821. Hitchin (Langley, Preston and Charlton
hamlets only) [HRO D/P 53 18/7].
1838. Essendon [HRO D/P 37 18/11].
1870. Welwyn (Woolmer Green only) [HRO
D/P 119 6/14].
1886. Hitchin (Preston hamlet only) [HRO
D/P 53 3/9].
1887, 1897. Aldenham [HRO D/P 3 1/14].

HUNTINGDONSHIRE

Abbreviations (see also page 12)
HUN = Huntingdon Branch of
Cambridgeshire Record Office.

All named
**1898, 1915, 1920, 1922, 1925. Steeple
Gidding** [HUN 2626/28/1, pp. 2, 60, 81, 92,
and 97].

Householders named with household numbers
1811, 1821. Alwalton [HUN 2716/11/1b and
2716/28/1].
1821. Godmanchester [HUN acc. no. 3915].
n.d. clearly 1821. Bluntisham [HUN
2611/18/5].

KENT

Abbreviations (see also page 12)
BCL = Bromley Central Library.
CCA = Canterbury Cathedral Archives.
FAO = Kent Archives Office (South East Kent area), Folkestone.
KAO = Kent Archives Office (now part of Centre for Kentish Studies), Maidstone.
LPL = Lambeth Palace Library, London.
ML = Kent County Library (now part of Centre for Kentish Studies), Springfield, Maidstone.
MM = Kent Arch. Soc. Library, Maidstone Museum.
SAO = Kent Archives Office (Medway area), Strood.

Publications
All named: 1676. Goodnestone next Wingham [CCA H/Z 82] in The Compton Census of 1676: a critical edition by E. A. Whiteman (1986), 635-44; Stansted [LPL VP 1C/9, ff. 79] in North West Kent F.H.S. jnl., 2 (7), 235 (1982).

Householders named with household numbers: 1757. Tunstall, in Bibliotheca Topographica Britannia no. 1: 'The history and antiquities of Tunstall in Kent', by E.R. Mores (1780), 105 (copy at ML, photocopies at KAO and CamGp).

1790. Hayes [BCL] in North West Kent F.H.S. jnl., 4 (4), 132-35 (Dec. 1986).

1801, 1811, 1821. Deal, par. St. Leonard [CCA] in Mfche copies publ. by Kent F.H.S. Rec. Publ. 177 (1985).

1801. Bromley [BCL 646] index publ. in North West Kent F.H.S. jnl., 1 (5) (1980).

1821. Beckenham [BCL 641] index publ. in North West Kent F.H.S. jnl., 1 (6) (1980).

All named with ages
1851-54, 1871, 1881, 1891. Goodnestone next Wingham (draft civil censuses, 1851 noting deaths to 1854) [CCA U3/232/19/7-10].

All named
1565. Eythorne and Waldershare (with children's ages) [KAO PRC 43/13/12]; Alkham, Charlton (in Dover) and Dymchurch [KAO PRC 43/13/1,8,10].
1676. Goodnestone next Wingham [CCA H/Z 82], copy at CamGp. published; Hackington [CCA H/Z 84], copy at CamGp; Stansted and Wrotham [LPL Compton Survey 1676. VP 1C/9, ff. 79,81-84], Stansted published.

All named continued

1695-1700 (every year). New Romney [KAO NR/RTb 1-6] (1,000 each year) copies of 1696, 1697, 1700 at CamGp.
1803. Folkestone [FAO Folkestone Borough Records CPm 6-9].
1805-07. Hunton (some children's ages) [KAO P197/18/1].
1883. Yalding (with children's ages) [KAO P408/28/1].
1896-1913. Bredhurst [KAO P44/28/1].

Householders named with household numbers
1565. Lympne and New Romney [CCA Q/C/1, 6].
n.d. clearly 1565. Burmarsh [KAO PRC 43/13/7].
n.d. c.1565. Canterbury, pars. St. Martin and St. Paul (document decayed at edges, some losses) [CCA CC E/Q 1].
1676. Boughton Malherbe [CCA H/Z 30], copy at CamGp.
1695. Brasted (town part only) [KAO P42/3/1].
1705. 36 pars. in Bewsborough, Cornilo, Downhamford, Eastry, Kinghamford, Preston, Ringslow, and Wingham hundreds in Wingham petty-div. [KAO Q/CTz 2] (6,000), copies at CamGp.
1757. Tunstall, see publications.
1776. East Malling [KAO P242/1/3A].
1790. Hayes [BCL], published.
1801,1811,1821. Deal, par. St. Leonard [Par. Recs. believed held uncatalogued at CCA] (1,340 names in 1811). Mfiche published (copies at KAO, CCA, and SoG).
1801, 1811. Borden [KAO P35/28/1, 2].
1801,1811. Smarden [KAO P339/18/2, 3].
1801. Bromley [BCL 646], index published; Eastry [CCA U11/6 folder 3]; Folkestone [FAO Fo/AZ 1/1, 2] (88); West Malling [KAO P243/28/1].
1810. Luddesdown [KAO P235/28/4].
1811. Canterbury Cathedral [CCA U3/100/11A/12]; Goudhurst [KAO P157/18/1 with transcript]; Lower Hardres [CCA U3/107/18/2]; Maidstone, par. All Saints (incomplete) [KAO P241/28/42].
1815. Wootton [CCA U3/136/28/2].
1821. Beckenham [BCL 641], index published; Penshurst [KAO P287/18/15/2]; Rochester, par. St. Nicholas [SAO P306/18/22] (518); Thanington [CCA U3/126/12/2 and Ts. copy] (original unfit for production).

Kent: *Householders* continued

1830. Dymchurch (some ages given) [KAO P125/18/14].

n.d. c.1830. Westwell [KAO P390/18/8].

1831. Horsmonden [KAO P192/18/9]; Ringwould [CCA U3/104/28/1]; Sellindge [KAO P329/18/3]; Shadoxhurst [MM transcript of lost original in Leland Duncan Mss. misc. vols., vol. 8]; Tenterden (household forms) [KAO P364/18/18].

1911. St. Nicholas at Wade [CCA U3/18/24/1/4-6].

Easter Books

1747-8, 1750. Margate, par. St. John Baptist [CCA U3/140/3/5/2 and U3/140/40/3/6].

Communicants Lists

1565 and n.d. c.1565. Bobbing, Bredgar, Brook, Brookland, Doddington, Ebony, Frinsted, Hamyshm(?), Littlebourne, Milton beside Sittingbourne, Newnham, Norton, Orlestone, Ospringe, Preston next Faversham, Queenborough, 'Sellynge', Sheldwich, Shoulden, Staplehurst, Stockbury, Stone, 'Stoure' (Sturry ?), Tunstall, Wormshill [KAO PRC 43/13/3-39], copy of Staplehurst at CamGp.

1565. Appledore, Fairfield, Milsted, Saltwood, Woodchurch [CCA Q/C/3-9]

1567. Appledore [KAO PRC 43/13/2].

1568. Wye [KAO PRC 43/13/40].

1590. Herne [KAO PRC 21/10/308], copy at CamGp.

LANCASHIRE

Abbreviations (see also page 12)

BCL = Bolton Central Library, Archives Dept.

CRO = Cheshire Record Office, Chester.

LA = Liverpool Athenaeum Library, Church Alley, Liverpool.

LCL = Liverpool Central Library, Record Office.

LRO = Lancashire Record Office, Preston.

MCL = Manchester Central Library, Archives Dept.

WCL = Warrington Central Library.

WiRO = Wigan Record Office, Leigh.

Publications

All named with ages: 1801. Winwick with Hulme [CRO P158/7/8] in *North Cheshire Family Historian*, 5 (1), 8-15 (Feb. 1978).

All named: 1676. Broughton (chapelry in par. Preston) [LRO ARR 31] in *Recusant History*, 15, 168-175 (1979-81).

All named: 1801. Turton (Edgeworth township only) [location of original unknown] in *Bolton Chronicle*, 24 Nov. 1906. Index in *Manchester and Lancashire Genealogist*, 11 (2), 12-13 (1975).

Householders named with household numbers: 1676. Bispham [location of original unknown, but Ts. copy at MCL] in *Proceedings, Fylde Hist. and Antiq. Soc.*, 1, 47-53 (Blackpool, 1940).

Householders named with household numbers: 1801. Bury (Elton township only) [LRO CBB/9] in *Manchester Genealogist*, 20 (4) and 21 (1) (1984-85).

All named with ages

1801. Winwick (Winwick with Hulme township only) [CRO P158/7/8], copy at CamGp, published.

All named with birthdates

1851-52. Winwick with Hulme [LRO DDX/153/5(3)].

All named

1676. Broughton (chapelry in par. Preston) [LRO ARR 31], copy at CamGp, published.

1701. Lowton (chapelry in par. Winwick) [WiRO D/P 17/24/4], copy at CamGp.

1801. Edgeworth, see publications.

1875-1901. Chatburn (with some birthdates) [LRO PR 3184/2/1].

1897-1912. Newchurch in Pendle (with some birthdates) [LRO PR 3182/14/7].

Lancashire *continued*

Householders named with household numbers
1676. Bispham [location of original unknown, but Ts. copy at MCL L1/55/3/2], published.
1764, 1832. Standish (all ten townships) [LRO PR 3134/2/7 (ff. 28+) and 12].
1798. Ormskirk (Scarisbrick township only) [LRO DDSc/26/46].
1801, 1811. Croston [LRO PR 2644, 2645].
1801. Bury (Elton township only) [LRO CBB/9], published; **Whalley** (Clitheroe township and borough only) [LRO MBC/650]; **Liverpool** (whole city/civil parish) [LA. Mf. copy at LCL Mf.7/14] (14,000) (see also analysis of this in *Trans. Hist. Soc. of Lancashire and Cheshire*, 130, 73-113 (1980)).
1811, 1821, 1831. Great Bolton (township in par. Bolton le Moors) [BCL ref:PGB with Mf. copies and Ts. indexes]. Mfiche indexes at SoG.
1811. Ashton under Lyne (including Stalybridge, Heyrod, Mossley and part Leizley townships) [LRO PR 2583] (3,042), copy at CamGp.
n.d. probably **1811. Wigan** (incomplete, about half of town) [WiRO AB/Misc] (1,300).
1821, 1831. Prescot (Penketh township only) [WCL MS.2020].
1821. Eccleston (Eccleston township only) [LRO PR 3052/14/2].
n.d. clearly **1821. Broughton** (chapelry in par. Preston) [LRO PR 1892/1, 2].
1831. Whalley (Clitheroe township and borough only) [LRO DDX/28/262] (888).
1905. Tockholes (chapelry in par. Blackburn) [LRO PR 2765/7].

LEICESTERSHIRE

Abbreviations (see also page 12)
DRO = Derbyshire Record Office, Matlock.
LRO = Leicestershire Record Office, Leicester.

All named with ages
1841-46 Shepshed (civil census with additions) [LRO DE 394/67].

All named with years of birth
1893-98. Evington [LRO DE 2636/67].

All named
n.d. clearly **1676. Great Glen** [LRO ID 41/43/60, 90] (one week's notice of production required).
1695. Rothley [LRO 44′28/970/1-9], copy at CamGp.
1695/6. Leicester, par. **St. Martin** [LRO BR.IV.2.7], copy at CamGp.
1697. Leicester, par. **St. Mary** [LRO BR.IV.2.6], copy at CamGp.
1699. Leicester, par. **St. Margaret** [LRO BR.IV.2.8], copy at CamGp.
n.d. clearly **1719. Anstey** (chapelry in par. Thurcaston) [LRO DE 1416/197].
n.d. clearly **1733. Thurcaston with Cropston** (excl. Anstey) [LRO DE 1416/196].
n.d. c.1846. **Bottesford** and **Normanton** (with children's birthdates) [LRO DE 829/114], copy at CamGp.
1852. Bottesford (with children's birthdates) [LRO DE 829/114], copy at CamGp.
1867. Bottesford, Easthorpe and **Normanton** (with children's ages) [LRO DE 829/114], copy at CamGp.

Householders named with household numbers
1801, 1811. Bruntingthorpe [LRO DE 2607/59, 60].
1801. Houghton on the Hill [LRO DE 2555/3/2].
n.d. clearly **1801. Thurcaston** (excl. Anstey) [LRO DE 1416/200/2].
1811. Loughborough (incomplete, half of town) [LRO DE 667/188]; **Market Harborough** [LRO DE 3184] (335); **Thurcaston** (excl. Anstey) [LRO DE 1416/200/1].
1814, 1821. Allexton [LRO DE 1819/26].
1814. Thurmaston South (chapelry in par. Belgrave) [LRO DE 2790/216].
1815. Billesdon [LRO DE 2492/25]; **Goadby** [LRO DE 2493/7].
1821. Lutterworth [LRO DE 2559/123, 124]; **Melton Mowbray** [LRO DG 25/20/2-4] (537); **Quorndon** [LRO 2 D 54].

Leicestershire: *Householders* continued

n.d. clearly **1821. South Kilworth** [LRO DE 209/12/19].
1831. Osgathorpe (incomplete) [LRO DE 1668/83].
1838. Netherseal (since 1891 in Derbyshire) [DRO D77M box 23, 'Books'].

Easter Books
1586-90. Leicester, par. **St. Mary** [LRO BR 111/8/24].
1593-1696. Thurcaston [LRO DE 1416/70, 71].
1707-12. Sapcote [LRO DE 933/24].
1728-78. Coleorton [LRO DE 1913/57].
1738-40. Leicester, par. **St. Margaret** [LRO transcript in 24 D65/0/4].

LINCOLNSHIRE

Abbreviations (see also page 12)
LAO = Lincolnshire Archives Office, Lincoln.

All named with birthdates
1857-70. Hagnaby (Lindsey) [LAO Hagnaby Par. 23].
1889-1909. Holbeach (Holland) [LAO Holbeach Par. 24/9, 10].

All named
1700. Sutterby (Lindsey) [LAO Lind. Dep. 35/2/7].
1771, 1791. Swinderby (Kesteven) [LAO Swinderby Par. 23/1, 10, with photocopy of 1771], copies at CamGp.
1850, 1853. Althorpe (Lindsey) (with children's ages) [LAO Althorpe Par. 23/2].
1859-60. Sutterton (Holland) (with children's ages) [LAO Sutterton Par. 23/21].

Lincolnshire continued

Householders named with household numbers
1755, 1762. Leverton (Holland) [LAO Leverton Par. 4/2, ff. 101-2 and 120-1], copy of 1762 at CamGp.
1801, 1811. Whaplode (Holland) [LAO Whaplode Par. 23/1].
1801. Little Ponton (Kesteven) [LAO Little Ponton Par. 1/2 and Mfiche copy].
1811, 1821, 1831. Fleet (Holland) [LAO Fleet Par. 23/5].
1811, 1821. Waddington (Kesteven) [LAO Waddington Par. 23/1].
n.d. clearly **1811. Winteringham** (Lindsey) (incomplete) [LAO Winteringham Par. 23/1].
1821, 1831. Canwick (Kesteven) [LAO Canwick Par. 23/1].
1821. Barnetby le Wold (Lindsey) [LAO Barnetby le Wold Par. 23/1]; **Lincoln** par. **St. Martin** [LAO Lincoln St. Martin Par. 19] (363); **Walcot by Folkingham** (Kesteven) [LAO Walcot by Folkingham Par. 23].
1831. Fillingham (Lindsey) [LAO Fillingham Par. 19/1]; **Gedney Hill** (Holland) [LAO Gedney Hill Par. 23/9]; **Grantham** (Kesteven) (whole parish except Westgate ward) [LAO Grantham Par. 23/6] (555).
1885. Ludborough (Lindsey) [LAO Ludborough Par. 23/1].
1890-98. Barton on Humber, par. **St. Mary** (Lindsey) [LAO Barton on Humber Par. 23/1].
1911. Whaplode (Holland) [LAO Whaplode Par. 23/10].

Communicants Lists
1650. Bonby (Lindsey) [LAO Bonby Par. 1/1 and Mfiche copy].
1683-89. Mareham le Fen (Lindsey) [LAO Mareham le Fen Par. 10/1].

LONDON

Abbreviations (see also page 12)
CLRO = Corporation of London Records Office.
GL = Guildhall Library, Dept. of Mss., London.

Publications

All named: 1695. London, 80 out of 97 parishes within the city walls [CLRO] indexed in London Inhabitants within the Walls, 1695, London Record Society, 2 (1966) (60,000 names). There is a separate index at CLRO to 54,000 names in 13 city parishes 'without the walls' (see below).
Householders named with household numbers: 1733, 1734. St. Mary Aldermary [GL Ms. 8991] in printed parish register in Harleian Soc. Registers, 5, 235-238 (1880).

All named

1695. City of London, 80 out of 97 parishes 'within the walls' and 13 parishes 'without the walls' [CLRO]. Indexes to whole collection, published (see above), copies, some parishes at CamGp. Parishes included 'without the walls': St. Andrew Holborn (part); St. Bartholomew: the Great, the Less; St. Botolph: without Aldersgate, Aldgate (part), Bishopsgate; St. Bride: Bridewell Precinct; St. Dunstan in the West; St. Giles without Cripplegate; St. Olave Southwark (London Bridge Precinct); St. Sepulchre; and Whitefriars Precinct. Parishes 'within the walls' which do not survive and therefore not indexed in London R.S. 2: Holy Trinity the Less; St. Nicholas: Acons, Cole Abbey, Olave; St. Olave: Hart Street, Jewry, Silver Street; St. Pancras Soper Lane; St. Peter: le Poer, upon Cornhill, Westcheap; St. Stephen: Coleman Street, Walbrook; St. Swithin London Stone; St. Thomas Apostle; St. Vedast Foster Lane.
1696. St. Benet and St. Peter Pauls Wharf [BL Add. Mss. 32645 ff. 4-11].
1704. St. Benet Sherehog [GL Ms. 7625].
1831. St Benet Pauls Wharf [GL Ms. 8935].

Householders named with household numbers
1733, 1734. St. Mary Aldermary [GL Ms. 8991], copy at CamGp. published.
1733. St. Thomas Apostle [GL Ms. 8991], copy at CamGp.
1801, 1821. St. Helen Bishopsgate [GL Ms. 6852 and 11, 419].

Householders continued

1801, 1811, 1821, 1831. St. Nicholas Acons [GL Ms. 4306].
1801, 1811, 1821. St. Sepulchre Holborn [GL Ms.3260/1-5].
n.d. c.1806. St. Benet and St. Peter Pauls Wharf [GL Ms. 8937].
1811, 1821. Allhallows Lombard Street [GL Ms. 10, 784 and 10, 785].
1811, 1821. St. Benet Pauls Wharf [GL Ms. 8933, 8934].
1811, 1821. St. Benet Sherehog [GL Ms. 7626, 7627].
1811, 1821, 1831. St. Mary Woolchurch Haw [GL Ms. 8110, 8131].
1811, 1821, 1831. St. Mary Woolnoth [GL Ms. 8109, 8128].
1811, 1821, 1831. St. Peter Cornhill [GL Ms. 4190].
1811, 1831. St. Peter Pauls Wharf [GL Ms 8932, 8932A].
1811, 1821. St. Swithin London Stone with St. Mary Bothaw [GL Ms. 566/1-2 and 3375/1-2].
1811, 1821, 1831. St. Thomas Apostle [GL Ms. 674].
1811. St. Ann Blackfriars (incomplete) [GL Ms. 7753]; St. Botolph Bishopsgate [GL Ms. 4523]; St. John Baptist Walbrook [GL Ms. 7618].
1821, 1831. St. Margaret Lothbury [GL Ms. 4620].
1821, 1831. St. Mary Abchurch [GL Ms. 3897].
1821. St. Katherine Coleman [GL Ms. 7723].
1831. St. Christopher le Stocks [GL Ms. 6146]; St. Clement Eastcheap [GL Ms. 3681]; St. Katherine Cree [GL Ms. 7697]; St. Matthew Friday Street [GL Ms. 7684]; St. Peter Westcheap [GL Ms. 7690].
1880. St. Peter le Poer and St. Benet Fink [GL Ms. 22, 509].

Communicants Lists

1673-74. St. Dunstan in the West [BL Harleian Mss. 1472, ff. 269].

MIDDLESEX

Abbreviations (see also page 12)

BpL = Brentford Public Library, Boston Manor Road.

CLS = Chelsea Library, Kings Road, SW3.

CSW = Chiswick Library, London Borough of Hounslow, Dukes Avenue, W4.

GLRO = Greater London Record Office.

GMB = The Grange Museum, London Borough of Brent, Neasden Lane, NW10.

HAD = Hackney Archives Dept, Rose Lipman Library, De Beauvoir Road, N1.

HFA = Hammersmith and Fulham Archives, Shepherds Bush Library, 7 Uxbridge Road, W12.

HpL = Harrow Local History Library, Civic Centre Library, Harrow.

LBB = London Borough of Barnet Library Services Archives, The Burroughs, Hendon, NW4.

MpL = Marylebone Library, Westminster City Libraries, Marylebone Road, NW1

SCL = Camden Local History Library, Swiss Cottage Library, 88 Avenue Road, NW3.

THL = Tower Hamlets Local History Library and Archives, Bancroft Library, 277 Bancroft Road, E1.

WCL = Westminster City Libraries (Archives and Local Studies), Victoria Library, 160 Buckingham Palace Road, SW1.

Publications

All named with ages: 1599. Ealing [PRO E163/24/35] in 'An Elizabethan Village Census', by K.J. Allison, in *Bull. Inst. Hist. Res.* 36, 91-103 (1963). Also in *Middlesex County Times*, 14 Feb. 1931. Also in *Ealing Local History Soc. Members Papers*, 2 (Oct. 1962).

Householders named with household numbers: 1810. New Brentford [BpL] in *West Middlesex F.H.S. jnl.*, 2 (2) (Spring 1981).

Householders named with household numbers: 1811. St. John at Hackney [HAD P/J/Misc II/1-6] indexed in *East of London F.H.S., Parish Returns Series*, 1, **Hackney**, 1811 (1988).

All named with ages

1599. Ealing [PRO E163/24/35], copy at CamGp, published.

All named

1695. Westminster, par. St. Margaret (St. Margaret's Long Ditch and Petty France wards, St. Peter ward and Palace ward only) [WCL E1566-69], copy at CamGp.

1699. Harefield [PRO T64/302], copy at CamGp.

Householders named with household numbers

n.d. c.1790. Westminster, par. St. George, Hanover Square [GLRO TC/St. G/1, 2 and Mf copy X45/1].

1801, 1811. Hampstead [SCL A/G/1, 2] (691 names in 1801; 842 names in 1811).

1801, 1811, 1821. Hendon [LBB] (450 names in 1821).

1801, 1811. Westminster, par. St. Margaret (mostly statistics but some householders' names given) [WCL E2867].

1801, 1811, 1821. Westminster, par. St. Mary le Strand [WCL G1050-52] (170 names in 1821).

1801. Chelsea, par. St. Luke [CLS] (1,637); Chiswick [CSW. copy at GLRO F 101] (556), copy at SoG; Westminster, par. St. James Piccadilly (Great Marlborough ward only) [WCL D1742], copy at SoG.

1810. New Brentford [BpL], published.

1811. St. John at Hackney [HAD P/J/Misc II/1-6 and Mf XP 208], Mf. copy at SoG. Index published.

1821, 1831. Hammersmith [HFA PAH/1/214, 215] (1,406 names in 1821; 1,712 names in 1831).

1821, 1831. Marylebone, par. St. Marylebone [MpL originals and Mf. copies] (9,761 names in 1821, 11,608 names in 1831).

1821, 1831. Poplar, par. All Saints [THL POP/750-55 and 756-67 and indexes].

1821, 1831. Willesden (1831 incomplete) [GMB acc. A50/1977 and A57/1977] (234 names in 1821).

1821. St. John at Hackney [HAD P/J/CW/124 and Mf. copy] (3,715); Westminster, par. St. Margaret (Absey and Grand wards only) [WCL E2865].

1831. Harrow [GLRO Harrow Parish records, Middx DRO 3/F 13/1-5] (609); St. John at Hackney [HAD P/J/Misc 1/1 and Mf. XP 208. Index in preparation] (5,220); Little Stanmore [HpL E1 Extra Oversize] (136).

Monmouthshire – see with Wales

NORFOLK

Abbreviations (see also page 12)
NRO = Norfolk Record Office, Norwich.

Publication
Householders and wives named with ages and household numbers: **1570. City of Norwich** (but confined to poor inhabitants, about 25% of population) [NRO Norwich City Records, case 20, shelf C] in *The Norwich Census of the Poor, 1570,* Norfolk Rec. Soc. **40** (1971) (1,400 names).

All named with ages
1821. Sparham [NRO NNAS safe 2, no. 30]; **Winfarthing** (very good) [NRO PD78/79].
1831. Alderford [NRO PD43/27].
1841, 1851. Bilney and **Beetley** (draft civil censuses) [NRO PD194/28].
1842. Heacham [original in church. Photocopy at NRO Acc. 29.6.1971 (R 152 C)].
1861,1871. Bedingham (Draft civil censuses) [NRO PD443/65].
1894, 1895. Forncett St. Peter [NRO PD421/97(S)].

All named with birthdates
1833-49. Foxley [NRO PD233/32].
1895-1920. Hunworth and Stody [NRO Acc. 9.4.1974 (R 191 D)].

All named
1704. North Walsham [NRO Pet. 574 99x3] (1,300).
1770. Blakeney [NRO PD619/31].
n.d. **c.1770. North Creake** (with some children's ages) [BL Althorp Papers E51].
1801, 1811. Winfarthing [NRO PD78/77, 78].
1801. Illington [NRO PD488/19].
1831. Coston [NRO PD320/20].
1843-47. Fulmodestone (with children's ages or birthdates) [NRO Acc. 4.7.1975 (T 189 D)].
1846. Burston [NRO PD101/37].
1869-86. Starston [NRO PD119/88].
n.d. **c.1895. Great Cressingham** and **Bodney** [NRO PD131/74, 75].
1930-43. Shelton (with some birthdates) [NRO PD358/40].

Householders named with household numbers
1557. Clackclose Hd. (23 parishes) [NRO PRA 652 (382x8)] (900), copy at CamGp (analysed in *Norfolk Archaeology*, **3**, 52-61, 'Presentments of grain with number of acres to sow and number of persons in each household').

Householders continued
1596. Clackclose Hd. (incomplete) [NRO PRA 653 (382x8)] (400), copy at CamGp.
1736, 1737, 1739. Shotesham All Saints [NRO FEL 870a 556x2], copies at CamGp.
1736, 1737. Shotesham St. Martin and **Shotesham St. Mary** [NRO FEL 870a 556x2], copies at CamGp.
1747. Wymondham [NRO PD184/3], copy at CamGp.
1768. Baconsthorpe and **Bodham** [NRO PD334/24 and copy in BUL4/327 606x2], copies at CamGp.
1777. Carleton Rode [NRO PD254/187], copy at CamGp.
1787. Northwold [NRO NAS 19117(P 153 F) schedule on map].
1788. Felbrigg [NRO WKC 7 4, 404x1].
1793. Wells next the Sea [original in church. Photocopy at NRO xerox, Gerken 19.9.1986 (R 152 C)].
1796. North Creake [BL Althorp Papers E51].
1800. Southrepps [NRO PD468/32].
1801, 1811, 1821. Baconsthorpe [NRO PD334/43].
1801, 1811. Winfarthing [NRO PD78/75].
1801. Beeston next Mileham [NRO PD377/31]; **Hethersett** [NRO PD41/108]; **Ingworth** [NRO PD521/36]; **Starston** [NRO PD119/124], copy at CamGp; **Thorpe next Norwich** (also known as Thorpe St. Andrew or Thorpe Episcopi) [NRO PD228/105], copy at CamGp; **Weston Longville** [NRO PD92/35]; **Woodton** [NRO PD57/51].
n.d. **c.1810. East Tuddenham** [NRO PD447/98].
1811, 1821. Old Buckenham [location of original unknown; copies at SoG and Norfolk and Norwich Gen. Soc.].
1811. Great Bircham [NRO PD34/43], copy at CamGp; **Wacton Magna** [NRO PD496/91].
1821. Bodham [NRO PD347/30]; **Bradfield** [NRO PD47/26]; **Diss** [NRO PD100/144], copy at CamGp; **Dunston** [NRO Dun(c) 80 499x6]; **Haddiscoe** [NRO PD208/134]; **West Harling** [NRO PD27/22]; **Tuttington** [NRO PD401/28]; **Wormegay** [NRO PC44/7].
1831. Norwich, par. St. John de Sepulchre [NRO PD90/86]; **Norwich, par. St. Peter Southgate** [NRO PD163/22].
1839. Gissing [NRO PD50/34]; **Tacolneston** (with ages of all inhabitants) [NRO PD148/60].

Norfolk: *Householders continued*

1842. Bawdeswell [NRO PD155/35 and Mf. 207/5], copy at CamGp.
1864-66. Norwich, par. St. Peter Parmentergate (with some ages) [NRO MS. 21713 513x4].
1887. Wreningham [NRO PD60/47].
1903-16. Norwich, par. St. John de Sepulchre [NRO PD90/82(S)].

Easter Books
1665-89. Kirby Cane [Bod MS.TOP. Norfolk f.1].
1754-82. South Lynn [NRO PD607/97].

Communicants Lists
1625-28. Shotesham [NRO FEL 915 556x7].
1632. Catfield [NRO NNAS Mf. 894718].
1682-84. Stalham [NRO PD262/1(S)].
1686-93. Norwich, par. St. Etheldreda [NRO PD4/52].
1729-40. Great Melton [NRO PD479/1].

NORTHAMPTONSHIRE

Abbreviations (see also page 12)
NRO = Northamptonshire Record Office, Northampton.

Publication
Householders named with household numbers: **1740. Aynho** [NRO 21P/114] in *Aynho: a Northamptonshire Village*, by N. Cooper, Appx. 3, 299 (Banbury Hist Soc., **20** (1984)).

All named with ages
1781. Great Brington, Little Brington and **Nobottle** [BL Althorp Papers G338], copy at CamGp.
1831. Evenley [NRO Misc. P'Stats 1223].

All named with birthdates
1587-1617. Courteenhall (with pedigree charts) [NRO 86P/6], copy at CamGp.

Northamptonshire *continued*

All named
1615, 1616, 1617, 1618, 1620, 1621, 1623, 1624, 1628. Cogenhoe [NRO 71P/1 with photocopy 755], copies at CamGp.
1697. Rothwell Hd. (22 parishes) [NRO Maunsell Colln. C(TM) 90, and Ts. copy in 'NRO Libr. 1433' with index], copies at SoG and CamGp.
1798. Great Billing [NRO 31P/225].
1822-59, 1834-69. Badby and **Newnham** (with children's ages or birthdays) [NRO 22P/78, 79].
1888. Harringworth (with children's ages) [NRO 156P/285].
1908. Thornhaugh and **Wansford** [NRO 319P/64].

Householders named with household numbers
1740. Aynho [NRO 21P/114], copy at CamGp, published.
1795. Lamport (incomplete) [NRO LHC 332].
1811. Great Billing [NRO 31P/226]; **Cold Ashby** [NRO 72P/45]; **Evenley** [NRO Misc. P'Stats 1222]; **Walgrave** [NRO 336P/41].
1815. Woodford Halse [NRO 372P/138].
1821. Braunston [NRO 46P/191, 192 and photocopy in 46P/251]; **Draughton** [NRO 107P/23]; **Eye** [NRO 121P/Mellows/1]; **Mears Ashby** [NRO 209P/97]; **Staverton** [NRO 300P/36]; **Woodford** [NRO 371P/77].
n.d. 1831?. Werrington (incomplete) [NRO 357P/114].
1833-78. Aynho [NRO 21P/1].
1848. Aldwinkle St. Peter (with householders' ages) [NRO NPL 1824].

Communicants Lists
pre-1612 and **1612. Cogenhoe** [NRO 71P/1 and photocopy 755], copies at CamGp.
1683, 1684. Stanwick [NRO 299P/14].
n.d. c.1770. Ashby St. Leger [NRO ASL 882].

NORTHUMBERLAND

Abbreviations (see also page 12)
NRO = Northumberland Record Office, North
Gosforth, Newcastle.
TWAS = Tyne and Wear Archives Service,
Newcastle.

All named
n.d. c.1816. Rothbury (though incomplete,
very detailed) [NRO EP103/114 and Mf.
copy in M595].
1830. Heddon on the Wall (all named except
servants) [NRO EP37/43 and Mf. copy in
M620].
1873-80. Alnwick, par. St. Paul (with ages of
most) [NRO EP5/19].
1891-92. Longframlington [NRO EP12/33].
1899. Heddon on the Wall (with children's
ages) [NRO EP37/43]

Householders named with household numbers
1811. Newcastle, par. All Saints (Byker only)
[TWAS 183/602 and Mf. 340], copy at
CamGp; Newcastle, par. All Saints
(Sandgate ward only) [TWAS 465/8 and Mf.
340], copy at CamGp.
1821. Newcastle, par. All Saints (Pilgrim ward
only) [TWAS 465/9 and Mf. 340], copy at
CamGp.
n.d. c.1845. Newcastle, par. St. Nicholas
(Tenison's Chapel district only) [NRO
EP86/68].
1848. Stamfordham [NRO EP76/52].
1858. Whitfield [NRO EP177/18 and Mf.
copy in M643].
1860. Benwell (par. created 1842 from
Newcastle, par. St. John) [TWAS 277/1 and
Mf. 308].
1890. Meldon [NRO EP152/9].
1894-95. Rothbury [NRO EP103/115].

Easter Books
1732-35. Morpeth [NRO EP28/99].

NOTTINGHAMSHIRE

Abbreviations (see also page 12)
NAO = Nottinghamshire Archives Office,
Nottingham.
NUL = Nottingham University Library, Mss.
Dept.

Publication
All named: 1676, 1688. Clayworth [NAO PR
5229] in *The Rector's Book, Clayworth*,
edited by H. Gill and E.L. Guilford
(Nottingham, 1910).

All named with ages
1851-54. Kinoulton (civil census with
additions) [NAO PR 24,220].

All named
1676, 1688. Clayworth [NAO PR 5229],
copies at CamGp and NUL [Misc. 258],
published.
1696. Hucknall Torkard [NAO PR 5363,
5363e], copy at CamGp.
1801. Welbeck [NAO DD 4P 68/74], copy at
CamGp.
1818. Strelley (with children's ages) [NAO
DDE 62/15], copy at CamGp.
1846. Caunton [NAO PR 6247], copy at
CamGp.
1861-68. North Wheatley (civil census with
additions) [NAO PR 3429].
1898, 1926-33. East Bridgford (some with
ages) [NAO PR 6533].

Householders named with household numbers
1794, 1811. West Retford [NAO PR 8024],
copies at CamGp.
1801. Eakring [NAO PR 8603]; Kinoulton
[NAO photocopy of original in private
collection in PR 17,048].
n.d. clearly 1803. Norwell [NAO PR 989].
1811, 1821. Kinoulton [NAO PR 15,341].
1811. Gotham [NAO PR 21,408]; Worksop
[NAO M420] (737).
n.d. clearly 1811. Laxton [NAO PR 4796/1].
1813. Radford [NAO PR 14,746], copy at
CamGp.
1815. Bilborough and Strelley [NAO DDE
14/75/1, 2], copies at CamGp.
1821. Gamston [NAO PR 20,745]; Laxton
[NAO PR 4142], copy at CamGp; Radford
[NAO PR 14,751-2], copy at CamGp.
n.d. clearly 1821. Hawton [NAO DDH
19/21], copy at CamGp;; Syerston [NAO PR
394]; Thorpe next Newark [NAO PR 5799].

Nottinghamshire: *Householders continued*

1824. Bleasby [NAO PR 6185], copy at CamGp.
1831. Beckingham [NAO PR 10,989]; **Blyth** [NAO PR 3743]; **Mansfield** [NAO DC/M 1/18/1] (1,889); **Walkeringham** [NAO PR 628, 629], copy at CamGp.
1832. Blyth (Barnby Moor and Bilby townships only) [NAO PR 19,556].
1845. Carlton on Trent [NAO DDVC 70/4], copy at CamGp.
n.d. c.1846 Wollaton [NAO PR 7763].
1849-51 Farndon and **Balderton** [NAO PR 21,789].
1878. Farnsfield [NAO PR 20,592].
1903-17 Nottingham, par. **St. Ann** [NAO PR 6786].

Easter Books
1595-1643. Sutton cum Lound [NAO PR 474].
1624. Nottingham, par. **St. Peter** [NAO M 23,973].
1668-1754. Kelham [NAO PR 10,598].
1742. Laxton [NAO PR 4076].
1768-75. Strelley [NAO PR 1629].
1794. Wiverton, Tithby, Cropwell and **Annesley** [NAO DD TB/3/2/10].

OXFORDSHIRE

Abbreviations (see also page 12)
OA = Oxfordshire Archives (formerly Oxfordshire Record Office), Oxford.

Publications
All named with children's ages: **1850.**
Banbury (Neithrop township only) [parish records in church] in *Banbury's Poor in 1850*, Banbury Hist. Soc. (1966), offprint from *Cake and Cockhorse* (jnl. Banbury Hist. Soc.), **3** (6) (Winter 1966).
Householders named with household numbers: **1801. Stoke Lyne** [OA MSS DD Par. Stoke Lyne d1] in *Oxfordshire F.H.S. jnl.*, **1** (9), 240 (1979).
1821. Wolvercote [OA MSS DD Par. Wolvercote b6] in *Oxfordshire F.H.S. jnl.*, **3** (3), 104 (1983).

All named with ages
1851. Standlake (draft civil census) [OA MSS DD Par. Standlake c11].
1861. Cowley [OA MSS DD Par. Cowley e6].
1881. Clifton Hampden [OA MSS DD Par. Clifton Hampden d6].
1881-84. Weston on the Green [OA MSS DD Par. Weston on the Green c3, ff. 93] (three latter are incumbent's visiting books giving different information to the civil censuses).

All named
1662. Oxford, par. **St. John Baptist** (incomplete) [Bod MS Wood E33 ff. 2-4].
1831. Stonesfield [OA MSS DD Par. Stonesfield b9].
1832. Oxford, par. **St. Giles** (Summertown only) [Bod MS. TOP Oxon. e240], copy at CamGp.
1850. Neithrop (Banbury), see publications.
1850-79. Mixbury [OA MSS DD Par. Mixbury c4].
1853-58. Garsington [OA MSS DD Par. Garsington a4].
1869-70, 1870, 1885-1901. South Leigh (with children's ages) [OA MSS DD Par. South Leigh e5 and b8, item r].
1893-97. Lower Heyford [OA MSS DD Par. Lower Heyford c8].

Householders named with household numbers
1742, 1771. Lower Heyford [Bod MS. TOP Oxon f50], copies at CamGp.
1751, 1795, 1811, 1821, 1831. Bletchingdon [OA MSS DD Par. Bletchingdon c7], copies at CamGp.

Oxfordshire: *Householders continued*

1789. South Weston [OA MSS DD Par. South Weston b2].

1801. Cottisford [OA MSS DD Par. Cottisford c2]; **Stoke Lyne** [OA MSS DD Par. Stoke Lyne d1], published.

1801, 1811, 1821. Stonesfield [OA MSS DD Par. Stonesfield b9].

1811. Rotherfield Greys [OA MSS DD Par. Rotherfield Greys c14]; **Yarnton** [OA MSS DD Par. Yarnton c2, ff. 74].

n.d. c.1813. Drayton St. Leonard (incomplete) [OA MSS DD Par. Drayton St. Leonard d5].

1814. Salford (also wives named) [OA MSS DD Par. Salford f1].

1820. North Newington [Bod MS. TOP Oxon d981, ff. 2].

1821. Begbroke (incomplete) [OA MSS DD Par. Begbroke c4]; **Britwell Salome** [OA MSS DD Par. Britwell Salome c5]; **Kiddington** [OA MSS DD Par. Kiddington c2]; **Wolvercote** [OA MSS DD Par. Wolvercote b6], published

1868. Albury [OA MSS DD Par. Albury b3].

1871-73, 1877, 1880, 1887. Shiplake (occasionally everybody named with children's birthdates) [OA MSS DD Par. Shiplake e3].

1879. South Leigh [OA MSS DD Par. South Leigh b8, item r].

1896, 1897. Tackley [OA MSS DD Par. Tackley c6, item b].

1898. Spelsbury [OA DIL 11/d/2].

Easter Books

1613-17, 1786-95. Cropredy [OA MSS DD Par. Cropredy c25/7 and c28].

1637-53. Shiplake [OA MSS DD Par. Shiplake c10].

c.1700. Cassington [OA MSS DD Par. Cassington c1].

1709-10, 1722. Middleton Stoney [OA MSS DD Par. Middleton Stoney b3].

Communicants Lists

1699-1723. Bucknell near **Bicester** [Bod MS. TOP Oxon e11].

RUTLAND

Abbreviations (see also page 12)
LRO = Leicestershire Record Office, Leicester.

Householders named with household numbers

1785, 1795. Ryhall and **Belmisthorpe** [LRO DE 2425/2, 3 and Mfiche copy].

SHROPSHIRE

Abbreviations (see also page 12)
HRO = Hereford and Worcester Record Office, Hereford.
NLW = National Library of Wales, Aberystwyth.
SLS = Shropshire Libraries: Local Studies Dept., Castle Gates, Shrewsbury.
SRO = Shropshire Record Office, Shrewsbury.

Publications

All adults named: **1675. Eaton under Heywood** [HRO HD Compton Census] in *The Compton Census of 1676: a critical edition* by E.A. Whiteman, 644-46 (1986).

All named with ages

1821. Wellington [SRO 3129/5/5, at present unfit for production, copy on card index in search room] (8,390).

All named

1695-1702 (every year). **Shrewsbury**, whole town and liberties [SRO 3365/275-79 with transcripts], copies of 1698-1702 at CamGp.

1772. Stockton (with children's ages) [SRO 3067/2/186].

1817-1822 (every year). **Longnor** [SRO 3961/Pa/6-11], copies at CamGp.

All adults named

1675. Eaton under Heywood [HRO HD Compton Census], copy at CamGp, published.

Shropshire *continued*

Householders named with household numbers
n.d. clearly **1676. Shelve** (incomplete) [HRO
HD Compton Census], copy at CamGp.
**1681. Kinnerley, Llanyblodwel, Llanymynech,
Melverley** and **Selattyn** [NLW
SA/Misc/1361-1482], copies at CamGp.
n.d. c.**1681. Knockin** [NLW
SA/Misc/1361-1482], copy at CamGp.
1686. Kinnerley, Knockin and **Selattyn** [NLW
SA/Misc/1361-1482], copies at CamGp.
n.d. **1680s, Oswestry, St. Martin** and
Whittington [NLW SA/Misc/1361-1482],
copies at CamGp.
1772-99. Donington [SRO 3793/Pa/1].
1801. West Felton [SRO 4687/Par/2, 3];
Longford [SRO 3264/1].
1808, 1812-1816 (every year). **Longnor** [SRO
3961/Pa/1-5], copies at CamGp.
1821, 1827. Shrewsbury, par St. Chad [SRO
1048/1076, 1077] (1,322 in 1821).
1821. Leighton [SRO 1286/100]; **Shrewsbury,
par. Holy Cross and St. Giles** [SLS] (299);
Shrewsbury, par. St. Mary [SRO 1041/C/1]
(1,050).
1831. Bishops Castle [SRO 552/22/89 and
transcript in 4232/1b] (388); **Shrewsbury,
par. St. Julian** [SRO 2711/P/54] (626).
1854. Meole Brace [SRO 4511/Par/1].
c.**1885-c.1900. Cardington** [SRO
3571/Gen/misc/2].

Easter Books
**1610-44, 1655-58, 1667, 1669-74, 1689-97,
1710-14. Morville** [SLS 9573b-j, 9661,
9662].
1649-1723, 1756-60. Madeley [SRO
2280/2/1-11].
1654, 1667-83. Aston Eyre (chapelry in par.
Morville) [SLS 9573a, 9573g].
1725-34, 1741-52, 1756, 1789-1880. Ludlow
[SRO 356/487; 2281/1/78, 79; 3834] (note:
Sue Wright – see Bibliography – says that
further Ludlow Easter Books for 1717-24,
1763-72, 1785-88, 1804-35 are held by
'Ludlow Historic Research Group' but does
not state where these are located).

SOMERSET

Abbreviations (see also page 12)
DRO = Dorset Record Office, Dorchester.
FM = Frome Museum.
SRO = Somerset Record Office, Taunton.
WRO = Wiltshire Record Office, Trowbridge.

All named with ages
1745. Trent (now in Dorset) [SRO photocopy
of original in private collection in
DD/X/Jones/1], copies at DRO and CamGp.
1821. Gasper (hamlet in par. Stourton, Wilts.)
[WRO 1240/38].
1827-29. Brislington [SRO DD/CO 8].

All named
1689. Blagdon [SRO D/P/blag 2/1/2].
1696, 1698. Wembdon (1698 incomplete)
[SRO D/P/wem 23/1].
1699. Wells (Southover only) [SRO DD/SAS
PR160].
1704. Langford Budville [SRO DD/SF 1869].
1831. Ston Easton [SRO DD/HI 294].
1866. Shipham [SRO D/P/ship 23/4].
n.d. c.**1875. Stowell** [SRO D/P/stow 2/9/4].
1879-1902. Barrington [SRO D/P/barr 2/9/1].
1901-09. Glastonbury, par. St. John [SRO
D/P/gla.j 9/5/1-3].
1914-19. Hambridge [SRO D/P/hamb 2/9/1].

Householders named with household numbers
n.d. c.**1720. Wookey** [SRO D/P/lav 23/1].
1740. Trent (now in Dorset) [SRO photocopy
of original in private collection in
DD/X/Jones/1], copies at DRO and CamGp.
1785. Frome [SRO photocopy of original in
private collection in T/PH/mas 2] (2,188),
copies at FM and CamGp.
1787, 1811. Camerton [BL Egerton Mss.
3121, ff. 91-96. Ts. copies at SRO], copies at
SoG and CamGp.
1801, 1811. Wincanton [SRO D/P/winc 23/2
and copies in DD/SAS SW4].
1801. Babcary [SRO D/P/bab 23/3]; **Huntspill**
[SRO D/P/hun 2/1/2].
1803. Monkton Combe [SRO DD/RG 69].
1803. Radstock [SRO D/P/rads 2/1/3], copy at
CamGp.
1811, 1821, 1829. Stowey [SRO D/P/sty 3/1/1].
1811. Ashcott [SRO D/P/ashc 23/1]; **Brockley**
[SRO D/P/broc 2/1/1]; **Chilton Polden** [SRO
D/P/chi.p 13/2/4]; **East Coker** [SRO
D/PC/cok.e 6/1/1]; **High Littleton** [SRO
D/P/lit.h 13/2/3]; **North Cadbury** [SRO
D/P/cad.n 4/1/3]; **Selworthy** [SRO D/P/sel
13/10/3].

35

Somerset: *Householders* continued

1821, 1831. Wedmore [SRO D/P/wed 23/4].
1821. Goathurst [SRO D/P/gst 23/4];
Montacute [SRO D/PC/mont 6/9]; **Tintinhull**
[SRO D/P/tin 23/3]; **Wrington** [SRO D/P/wri
23/1].
1882-84. Combe St. Nicholas [SRO
D/P/com.n 23/11].

Easter Books
1600. Drayton [SRO DD/SAS c/1696 6/24].
1605, 1607-09. West Pennard [SRO
DD/SAS/SE 36].
1743-50. Mells [SRO DD/SAS c/795 ML142].

STAFFORDSHIRE

Abbreviations (see also page 12)
BRL = Birmingham Reference Library,
Archives Dept.
LJRO = Lichfield Joint Record Office.
SRO = Staffordshire Record Office, Stafford.
WDL = Wednesbury District Library.
WLHC = Walsall Local History Centre.

Publications
All named: **1532-33. Archdeaconry of
Stafford**, most parishes [LJRO B/A/27ii] in *A
list of families in the Archdeaconry of
Stafford* , edited by A.J. Kettle, Staffordshire
Rec. Soc. Collections for the History of
Staffordshire, 4th. ser., **8** (1976) (51,000
names).

All named with ages
n.d. **c.1695. Lichfield** (whole city except
Cathedral Close) [BL Harleian Mss. 7022, ff.
1-42. Mf. copy at SRO in Mf. 38. Photocopy
at LJRO], copy at CamGp. Analysis by
compiler, Gregory King, of 12 Aug. 1695 at
BL Harleian Mss. 6839, ff. 28.
1701. Stoke upon Trent (Clayton, Fenton
Culvert, Hanley, Seabridge, Shelton and
Stoke upon Trent townships only) [SRO
D(W) 1742/55], copy at CamGp.
1851. Aston by Stone (not for civil census,
gives house owners) [SRO D4390/9/1].

Staffordshire *continued*

All named with birthdates
1861, n.d. **c.1880, 1893-98. Weston under
Lizard** [SRO D1060/2/1, 2, 3].

All named
1532-33. Archdeaconry of Stafford (most
parishes) [LJRO B/A/27ii] (51,000), copy of
par. Brewood at CamGp, published.
1693-98. Eccleshall (very detailed) [LJRO
B/A/21 with Ts. copy], copy at CamGp.
1695. Bilston [SRO D667/3/1], copy at
CamGp.

Householders named with household numbers
1622. Stafford (whole town) [SRO D1721/1/4
ff.154d-158], copy at CamGp.
1779, 1801. Biddulph [SRO D3539/1/48],
copy of 1779 at CamGp.
1801, 1811, 1821. Wednesbury [SRO
D4383/6/8/1, 2, 3; photocopies at WDL]
(1,194 names in 1821).
1801. Lichfield, par. St. Michael [LJRO
D27/9/4]; **Stafford, par. St. Mary** (Marston
township only) [SRO D53/A/P2/1]; **Walsall**
(whole civil parish, incl. Bloxwich, and
Bentley) [WLHC P312 with photocopies and
indexes] (1,984 names).
1811, 1821, 1831. Walsall (Borough township
only) [WLHC P312 with photocopies and
indexes].
1811. Colwich [SRO D24/A/PO 3362-64];
Newcastle under Lyme (whole town) [SRO
D3251/9/1] (1,245).
1820. Tettenhall [SRO D571/A/PO/165, 166].
1828. Lichfield, par. St. Chad (also known as
Stowe) (with householders' ages) [LJRO
D29/2/1].
1831. Blymhill [SRO D1044/7/2]; **Lichfield,
par. St. Mary** (incumbent's visiting book, not
for civil census) [BRL 241103 IIR 42].
n.d. **c.1831-33. Sedgley** [SRO D3319/3/1],
copy at CamGp.
1901-1928 (many lists) **Drayton Bassett and
Canwell** [SRO D3396/10/1, 2].

Easter Books
1555. Burton on Trent [SRO D(W)
1734/2/3/21B], copy at CamGp.

SUFFOLK

Abbreviations (see also page 12)
BRO = Bury St. Edmunds Branch, Suffolk Record Office.
LRO = Lowestoft Branch, Suffolk Record Office.
NRO = Norfolk Record Office, Norwich.
SRO = Suffolk Record Office, Ipswich.

All named with ages
1821, 1831. Westley [BRO FL647/7/5, 6].

All named
1695. Bury St. Edmunds, par. St. James [BRO 508/1], copy at CamGp; **Ubbeston** [SRO FC69/A1/1].
1788, 1789, 1790, 1791, 1797. Barham (some with ages, particularly in 1797) [SRO FB35/A3/1], copies at CamGp.
1857. Framlingham (some with ages) [SRO HD 266/1].
1862-79. Hitcham (with years of birth) [BRO FL586/13/4].

Householders named with household numbers
1743. Harkstead [SRO FB184/C1/1].
1753. Fressingfield [SRO FC90/C1/34], copy at CamGp.
1759. Withersdale [SRO FC90/C1/34], copy at CamGp.
1785. Copdock [NRO Wals XXXV/6 (R 190A)], copy at CamGp.
1799. Mildenhall (incomplete ?) [BRO 996/7/1].
1801, 1811, 1821. Ipswich, par. St. Clement [SRO FB98/G7/1, 2, 3] (916 names in 1821).
1801, 1811, 1831. Ipswich, par. St. Peter [SRO FB101/G11/1, 2, 3] (323 names in 1831) copies at CamGp.
1801, 1831. Brome [SRO FB127/A1/2 pp. 103-4].
1801. Holton St. Mary [SRO FB73/A1/1]; **Horringer** [BRO HD 901/1]; **Walsham le Willows** [BRO FL646/7/73]; **Worlingworth** [SRO FC94/G8/1].
1809. Clare [BRO FL501/1/51].
1811, 1821, 1831. Wickhambrook [BRO EL169/7/31 (1, 2, 7-14)].
1811. Glemsford [BRO FL575/13/1]; **Metfield** [SRO FC91/G7/1], copy at CamGp.
n.d. clearly **1811. Swilland** [SRO FB33/G1/1].
1818. Hopton [BRO FL588/7/57].
1821, 1831. Lowestoft [LRO 13/1, 2 and photocopies (1831 indexed)] (756 names in 1821).

Householders continued

1821. Aldham [BRO FB68/G1/1]; **Troston** [BRO FL643/7/5]; **Wetherden** [SRO HA87/K1/1/1].
n.d. clearly **1821. Glemsford** [BRO FL575/13/2]; **Pettistree** [SRO FC104/G15/3]; **Playford** [SRO FC22/A5/1].
1831. Athelington and **Cretingham** [SRO FB51/A4/1]; **Ipswich,** par. St. Margaret [SRO FB93/G6/1-6] (906), copy at CamGp.
1839. Kentford [BRO FL596/1/1b p.9].
1842-45. Hadleigh [SRO HD 358/1].
n.d. c.**1880. Coddenham** (householders' ages given) (incomplete) [SRO HA24:50/19/4, 5(4)].
1884. Fakenham [BRO FL569/1/3].

Householders named with all over age 16 labelled
1675. Worlingham (for Bishop Compton Census) [LRO FC1/A2/1].

Easter Books
1709-48. Lowestoft and **Gunton** [NRO PD589/80].

SURREY

Abbreviations (see also page 12)
CCL = Croydon Central Library, Local History Dept.
GL = Guildhall Library, London
GLRO = Greater London Record Office.
GMR = Guildford Muniment Room, Surrey Record Office.
LAD = Lambeth Archives Dept., Minet Library.
SLSL = Southwark Local Studies Library.
SRO = Surrey Record Office, Kingston.

Publications
All named **1801. Chobham** [SRO P34/17/1] in *Root and Branch*, jnl. West Surrey F.H.S., **13** (4), 132-3 (Spring 1987) and **14** (1), 16-18 (Summer 1987).
Householders named with household numbers **1801. Ewhurst** [SRO P38/3/291] in *Root and Branch*, jnl. West Surrey F.H.S., **12** (2), 65-67 (Autumn 1985); **Newdigate** [GMR PSH/NE/9/1] in *Root and Branch*, jnl. West Surrey F.H.S., **6** (3).
Mfiche index to **1811. Croydon**, for sale by East Surrey F.H.S. 'Record Publications M3' (1989).
Surrey Inhabitants Lists, 3rd edn. compiled by Cliff Webb, published (for sale) by West Surrey F.H.S. *Research Aids Series*, **7** (1991). Also see 'Early Census... Records in Surrey' by S. Gallagher, jnl. *East Surrey F.H.S.*, **12** (2) (Aug. 1989).

All named
1801. Chobham [SRO P34/17/1], published.
1851, 1861. Ewhurst (civil census drafts) [GMR PSH/EWH/20/1], Ts. indexes with West Surrey F.H.S.
1852. Compton [GMR PSH/COM/19/5, 6].

Householders named with household numbers
1788. Clapham [GLRO P95/TRI 1/72 and Ts. copy in R358].
1801, 1811. Bletchingley [SRO 2727/1/48/84, 86].
1801, 1811, 1821. Clapham [GLRO P95/TRI 1/73 and Ts. indexes in R358], Ts. indexes at SoG, copies at East Surrey F.H.S. and West Surrey F.H.S.
1801, 1811, 1821. Mortlake [SRO 2397/6/42, 43, 44] (403 names in 1821).
1801, 1811, 1821. Oxted [SRO P3/5/114, 117], copies at CamGp.

Householders continued
1801. Ewhurst [SRO P38/3/291 with Ts. index], published; **Guildford** [GMR 93/1] (464), copies at GL, SoG and West Surrey F.H.S; **Newdigate** [GMR PSH/NE/9/1], published.
1811, 1831. Chobham [SRO P34/17/2, 3], copies at West Surrey F.H.S.
1811. Croydon [CCL], Ts. index at GL and SoG., copies at East Surrey F.H.S. and West Surrey F.H.S. Mfiche index published; **Mitcham** [SRO 2553/7 with Ts. index], Ts. index at GL and SoG; **Southwark, par. St. Saviour** [GLRO P92/SAV/1473; index at SLSL] (2,547).
n.d. **1811?. Stoke D'Abernon** (excluding Oxshott) [SRO P53/4/17].
1815. Frimley [SRO 2589/9/2].
1821. Southwark, par. Christ Church (west division only) [GLRO P92/CTC/416, 424 and Mf. copy in X15/158. Index at SLSL]; **Thursley** [SRO P46/3/1], copy at West Surrey F.H.S.
1831. Newington, par St. Mary [SLSL (original unfit for production) index, giving all names, in 929.01 St.MN]; **Southwark, par. Christ Church** [SLSL Ms.80F and index in 929.01 CHR]; **Southwark, par. St. Saviour** [SLSL Ms.202-211 and index in 929.01 St.S]; **Streatham** [LAD P/S/3/13 with index].
1896-99. Battersea, par. St. Stephen [GLRO P70/STE/30-34].

Communicants Lists
1620-22. Southwark, par. St. Saviour [GLRO P92/SAV/187-315].

SUSSEX

Abbreviations (see also page 12)
ESRO = East Sussex Record Office, Lewes.
WSRO = West Sussex Record Office,
Chichester.

Publications

All original **1801-31** civil censuses giving names at ESRO have been published with indexes (1988-90) by PBN Publications, available from them at 22 Abbey Road, Eastbourne, Sussex, BN20 8TE (send S.A.E. or 2 I.R.C's for quotation): **Chiddingly 1821** (1990); **East Dean, 1831** (1989); **Hailsham, 1821** (1990); **Hailsham, 1831** (1990); **Hartfield, 1821** (1990); **Hastings, St. Clement, 1831** (1988); **Hastings, St. Mary, 1821** and **1831** (1990); **Lewes, St. John sub Castro, 1831** (1989); **Lewes, St. Michael, 1811** with jury list **c.1827** and voters list **c.1832** (1990); **Ticehurst, 1801** (1990); **Uckfield, 1831** (1988) and **Ticehurst '1831'** (1989). This last publication was found to be erroniously dated 1831, but is actually for Ticehurst for 1811 and part, 1821 – an errata slip has been inserted.
All named: **1863. Ewhurst** [ESRO PAR 324 7/5] in *Ewhurst Householders, 1863*, published with index (1991) by PBN Publications (as above).
Householders and wives named with ages and household numbers: **1838 Withyham** [ESRO PAR 512 7/1/1] in *Withyham Inhabitants, 1838*, published (1991) by PBN Publications (as above).

All named with ages

1821. Chiddingly [ESRO PAR 292 37/1], published; **Tangmere** [WSRO Add.Ms. 37864].

All named

1803. Kirdford [WSRO Par 116/37/1].
1821. East Hoathly [ESRO photocopy of original in Yale University Library in AMS 6093/2].
1822-29. Rusper (with children's birthdates) [WSRO Par 163/7/2].
1831. East Dean [ESRO PAR 304 37/3], published.
1837-51. Graffham and **Woolavington** (with years of birth) [WSRO Par 93/7/2].
1847-56. South Stoke [WSRO Par 185/7/3].
1852-58. Singleton (with years of birth) [WSRO Par 174/7/1].

All named continued

1863. Ewhurst [ESRO PAR 324 7/5], published.
1870-79. Upper Beeding (with children's ages) [WSRO Par 16/7/5].
1890. Salehurst [ESRO PAR 477 26/8].

Householders named with household numbers

1740. Chichester [WSRO Ts. copy from original in archives of Duke of Richmond and Gordon, Goodwood House, in 'Lists and Indexes No. 7'], copy at CamGp.
1784. Chichester [WSRO copy from original in unknown location in MP 414 with index].
1801. Ticehurst [ESRO PAR 492 30/3], published.
1803. Hurstpierpoint [WSRO Par 400/36/20, 21].
1811, 1821. Hurstpierpoint [WSRO Par 400/37/74-78].
1811. East Grinstead [WSRO Par 348/26/2/6 with copy and index in MP 2394]; **Kirdford** [WSRO Par 116/37/1]; **Lewes, par. St. Michael** [ESRO PAR 414 37/2/1], published; **Rusper** [WSRO Par 163/37/3]; **Ticehurst** [ESRO PAR 492 37/114, 117-120], published (as '1831').
1815. Fernhurst and **North Ambersham** [WSRO Par 82/7/2].
1821, 1831. East Grinstead (both incomplete) [WSRO Par 348/26/2/7-10].
1821, 1831. Hailsham [ESRO PAR 353 (acc.1333)], both published.
1821. Greatham [WSRO Par 209/7/3]; **Hartfield** [ESRO PAR 360 15/2/1], published; **Hastings, par. St. Mary in the Castle** (Inbounds only) [ESRO PAR 369 7/1, 2], published; **Ticehurst** (incomplete) [ESRO PAR 492 37/115], published (as '1831').
1831. Hastings, par. St. Clement [ESRO PAR 367 37/2/18, 20], published; **Hastings, par. St. Mary in the Castle** (Inbounds and Outbounds) [ESRO PAR 369 7/4-7], published; **Lewes, par. St. John sub Castro** [ESRO PAR 412 37/13/2, 3], published; **Uckfield** [ESRO PAR 496 26/15], published.
1838. Withyham (householders and wives named with ages) [ESRO PAR 512 7/1/1], published.
1908-18. East Dean and **Friston** [ESRO PAR 304 26/5].

39

WARWICKSHIRE

Abbreviations (see also page 12)
BRL = Birmingham Reference Library, Archives Dept.
CRO = Coventry City Record Office.
ROB = copies held by Mrs. Barbara Robinson, of 137 Gretna Road, Coventry, West Midlands CV3 6DS. She has transcribed and indexed almost all the local censuses for Warwickshire, and will make name searches for enquirers on receipt of S.A.E. (overseas, 2 I.R.Cs). A small fee may also be charged.
RpL = Rugby (East Divisional) Library.
SBT = Shakespeare Birthplace Trust Record Office, Stratford upon Avon.
WRO = Warwickshire Record Office, Warwick.

All named with ages
1684, 1781. Chilvers Coton [WRO CR 136 vol. 12 and CR 1841/23], copies at CamGp and ROB.
1782. Astley [WRO CR 1841/40], copies at CamGp and ROB.
1821. Stivichall [WRO DR 331/37/299], copy at ROB; **Tanworth** [WRO DRB 19/180], copy at ROB.
1875-1908. Stoneleigh [WRO DR 318/81].

All named
1698. Fenny Compton [WRO DR 103/7], copy at ROB (analysed in 'A Census of a Warwickshire village in 1698' by P. Styles, Birmingham Hist. Jnl. 3, 33-51).
1811. Barston [WRO DRB 46/87], copy at ROB.
1840. Bishops Tachbrook [WRO CR 1908/231/1-12], copy at ROB.
1864-74. Stoneleigh [WRO DR 318/80].
1873-76. Lighthorne and **Chesterton** (with children's ages) [WRO DR 220/3].

Householders named with household numbers
1522/3. Coventry (10 wards) [CRO Borough Archives Corporation Administrative Records: Taxation: W1405 (3 wards) and 263/2 (7 wards)], copy at CamGp (analysed in *Desolation of a city: Coventry and the urban crisis of the late middle ages*, by C.V. Phythian-Adams (1979)).
1751. Hatton (Beausale township only) [WRO DR 123/19], copy at ROB.
1765. Stratford upon Avon [SBT ER 1/8 pp. 507-525. Mf. copy at WRO in Z 384(sm)], copies at CamGp and ROB.

Householders continued
1801. Brinklow [WRO DR 366/210/2], copy at ROB; **Church Lawford** [WRO DR 309/2/2], copy at ROB; **Hillmorton** [WRO DR 256/37], copy at ROB.
1811, 1821, 1831. Coleshill [WRO DRB 100/127-130].
1811, 1821, 1831. Warwick, par. **St. Mary** [WRO DR 126/858-861], copies at ROB.
1814. Seckington [WRO DR(B) 22/6], copy at ROB.
1821. Austrey [WRO DRB 48/108], copy at ROB; **Barston** [WRO DRB 46/88]; **Bedworth** [WRO DR 225/411], copy at ROB; **Farnborough** [WRO DR 299/16], copy at ROB; **Kineton** [WRO DR 212/194], copy at ROB; **Rugby** [RpL. transcript at WRO B.Rug.Bil (P)], copies at CamGp and ROB; **Sheldon** [BRL DRO 42, box 6, Sheldon parish, no. 3], copy at ROB; **Southam** [in private collection but transcript at WRO Z 585 (sm) and Mfiche 31], copy at SoG.
1831. Arrow (Oversley township only) [WRO DR 734/40], copy at ROB; **Astley** [WRO DR 19/629], copy at ROB; **Bidford** [WRO HR 71/43], copy at ROB; **Bulkington** [at present untraced but copied by ROB at WRO]; **Halford** [WRO DR 362/61], copy at ROB; **Kingsbury** [WRO DR(B) 3/124, 125], copy at ROB; **Stratford upon Avon** (Borough only) [SBT BRT 8/274] (683); **Old Stratford** [SBT BRT 9/234] (330); **Warwick**, par. **St. Nicholas** [WRO DRO 115/223], copy at ROB.
1836. Chilvers Coton [WRO DR 374/99], copy at ROB.
1839. Bilton [WRO DR 221 box 7].
n.d. c.1860. Southam [WRO DR 583/179a], copy at ROB.
1913. Great Alne [WRO DR 344/36].

Easter Books
1594, 1595, 1613. Coventry, par. **St. Michael** [CRO Corporation Financial Records pre-1835, Rates: St. Michaels 9a].

WESTMORLAND

Abbreviations (see also page 12)
CRO = Cumbria Record Office, Carlisle.
KRO = Kendal Branch, Cumbria Record Office.
In this county townships are known as constablewicks, here abbreviated to 'c'wick'.

Publications
All, or householders, named: **1787.
Westmorland**, in *Vital Statistics: The Westmorland 'Census' of 1787*, compiled on order of Quarter Sessions, surviving returns for 44 c'wicks (as detailed below), edited by L. Ashcroft with introduction and indexes, published by Cumbria R.O. (Kendal), 1992.
All named: **1861. Crosby Ravensworth**, draft civil census with additions, detailed in *Roots and Records: when Sutherland came to Lakeland* by D.T. Jackson (Heversham, 1989), the original document being in the private possession of the author, as of Birk Nott, Heversham, Cumbria.

All named
1695. All pars. in Lonsdale ward, with Highgate, Stramongate and Stricklandgate in town of Kendal [KRO WD/Ry box 32, with indexes], copies at CamGp.
1787. Appleby, par. **St. Lawrence** (Colby c'wick); **Appleby**, par. **St. Michael** (Hilton and Murton c'wicks); **Askham** (Askham c'wick); **Barton** (Barton, Hartsop and Patterdale, Martindale and Sockbridge c'wicks); **Brough** (Stainmore c'wick); **Brougham** (Moorhouses and Woodside c'wick); **Cliburn** (Cliburn c'wick); **Clifton** (Clifton c'wick); **Crosby Ravensworth** (Birkbeck Fells and Reagill c'wicks); **Dufton** (Dufton c'wick); **Kirkby Stephen** (Kaber c'wick); **Kirkby Thore** (Milburn, Milburn Grange and Temple Sowerby c'wicks); **Longmarton** (Longmarton, Brampton and Knock c'wicks); **Lowther** (Lowther, and Hackthorpe and Whale c'wicks); **Morland** (Morland, Bolton, Kings Meaburn, Newby and Great Strickland c'wicks); **Newbiggin** (Newbiggin c'wick); **Warcop** (Burton and Sandford c'wicks) [KRO WQSP/C], copies at CamGp, published.
1888. Ambleside (with children's ages) [KRO WPR/63].

Householders named with household numbers
1683. Grasmere (with some ages) [CRO D/LONS/W1/31 pp. 122-3], copy at CamGp.
1787. Askham (Helton Flecket c'wick); **Bampton** (Bampton c'wick); **Crosby Ravensworth** (Crosby Ravensworth and Maulds Meaburn c'wicks); **Kendal** (Stricklandgate and Whinfell c'wicks); **Lowther** (Melkinthorpe c'wick); **Morland** (Little Strickland and Thrimby c'wicks); **Shap** (Shap, Keld, Thornship, Talebert and Racet, Hardendale and Rosgill with Sleddale c'wicks); **Warcop** (Bleatarn c'wick) [KRO WQSP/C], copies at CamGp, published.
1801, 1811. Beetham (Beetham and Farlton, and Haverbrack c'wicks) [KRO WPR/43].
1811. Crosby Ravensworth [KRO WPR/7].
1886, 1888-93, 1897, 1902. Cowgill (9 lists) [KRO WPR/69].

WILTSHIRE

Abbreviations (see also page 12)
WRO = Wiltshire Record Office, Trowbridge.

All named with ages
1801. Box [WRO 1719/78].
1821. Stourton (and Gasper, Somerset) [WRO 1240/38].

All named with birthdates
1834-36. Bowerchalke (very good) [WRO 1280/17].
1847-76. Compton Chamberlayne (the most detailed 'incumbents' visiting book' in Britain) [WRO 1256/1], copy at CamGp.

All named with baptismal dates
1785. Little Cheverell [WRO 1725/14].

All named
1695. Donhead St. Mary [WRO 980/2], copy at CamGp.
1697-1705. Kingsbridge Hundred parishes as follows: **Broad Hinton** (Binknoll tithing) **1697, 1700, 1701; Chisledon 1697; Chisledon with Draycot Foliatt 1700, 1702, 1705; Cliffe Pypard 1697, 1701; Hilmarton** (except Catcomb tithing) **1697, 1700, 1701;**

Wiltshire: *All named continued*

1697-1705. Liddington 1697, 1700, 1702; Lydiard Tregoze 1697, 1700, 1701; Lyneham 1697, 1700, 1701, 1702; Swindon 1697, 1701, 1702, 1705; Tockenham 1697, 1700, 1701; Wanborough 1697, 1700, 1702, 1705; Wootton Bassett 1697, 1701, 1702, 1705; Little Hinton 1700; Wroughton 1700, 1701; Wroughton (Kingsbridge five tithings) **1697; Wroughton** (Elcombe and Uffcott tithings) **1705** [WRO 212B/7202A/1-16 and some transcripts in 130/77/8 and WRO Library], copies at CamGp.
1858-60. Donhead St. Andrew [WRO 1732/21].
1886. East and West Harnham [WRO 1045/22].
1913-25. Chitterne All Saints [WRO 1109/15].

Householders named with household numbers
1744. Stanton St. Bernard [WRO 495/1], copy at CamGp.
1770. Steeple Ashton [WRO 730/288], copy at CamGp.
1787. Chisledon [WRO 1178/273 and copy], copy at SoG.
1800, 1813-27. Steeple Ashton and **Semington** [WRO 730/288], copies at CamGp.
1801. Horningsham [SoG copy of original in Longleat House Archives, Warminster]; **Keevil** (Bulkington tithing only) [WRO 653/30].
1803. Box [WRO 1719/30].
1811. Foxley [WRO 592/1]; **Grittleton** [WRO 1620/31]; **Woodborough** WRO 1737/5].
1821, 1831. Sutton Veny [WRO 949/21].
1821. Stratford sub Castle [WRO 1076/63]; **Trowbridge** [WRO 206/119] (1,786), copy at CamGp.
1826, 1827. Steeple Ashton [WRO 730/24, 25].
1831. Bromham [WRO 518/21]; **Downton** (Borough only) [WRO 2029/2]; **Stockton** (incomplete) [WRO 384/6]; **Stourton** [WRO 1240/39].
1887. Woodford [WRO 1987/16].
1891-1907. Broadchalke [WRO 1261/24].

Easter Books
1574-1607. Salisbury, par. St. Thomas [WRO 1900].
1634-40. Salisbury, par. St. Martin [WRO 1899].

WORCESTERSHIRE

Abbreviations (see also page 12)
DBL = Dudley Borough Library.
GRO = Gloucestershire Record Office, Gloucester.
SHRO = Hereford and Worcester Record Office, St. Helen's Branch, Worcester.
WRO = Hereford and Worcester Record Office, Headquarters at County Hall, Worcester.

Publications
All named: **1827. Blockley** (now in Gloucestershire) in *Guide to Blockley* by Revd. W.T. Eyre (1827), copies at GRO in PA52/3 and P52/MI 17.

All named
1827. Blockley, see publications.
1831. Wolverley [WRO 265.91:BA 1693/2 and Mf.X965.91].
1838. Elmley Lovett (incomplete) [SHRO 850:BA 9845/5(i)].

Householders named with household numbers
1631. Claines (Whistones tithing only) [SHRO 705.753:BA 7811/4], copy at CamGp.
1795. Worcester, par. St. Andrew [SHRO 850:BA 4426/3(iii)], copy at CamGp.
n.d. clearly **1801,** with **1811** and **1831. Kidderminster,** par. St. Mary (foreign, part outside borough, only) [SHRO 850:BA 4766/8(i)].
1811, 1821. Bromsgrove [WRO 491:BA 10,059/178(iii), 179 and Mf.X949.1] (1,378 in 1811; 1,513 in 1821).
1819. Childs Wickham (with householders ages) [SHRO 705.962:BA 8965/10(i) 5, 6].
1821. Bewdley [WRO 498:BA 8681/234(v) 3-34] (879); **Himbleton** [SHRO b850:BA 4087/5(v)]; **Kidderminster,** par. St. Mary (part of borough only) [SHRO 850:BA 4766/8(i)]; **Ripple** [SHRO 850:BA 9422/9(ii) 1]; **Worcester,** par. St. John in Bedwardine [SHRO 850:BA 1671/9] (482).
1831. Belbroughton [DBL Earls of Dudley Colln]; **Tardebigge** [SHRO b850:BA 8552/4].
1899, 1905, 1907. Cleeve Prior [SHRO 850:BA 9048/7(ii)3-10].
1900, 1907. Elmley Lovett [SHRO 850:BA 9845/15(x) 2, 3].
1905, 1910. Little Witley [SHRO 850:BA 8936/(vii) 5, 6].

YORK and the AINSTY

Abbreviations:
BI = Borthwick Institute, York.
YAO = York City Archive Office.

All named with ages
1861. **Bishopthorpe** (Middlethorpe township only) (draft civil census) [BI PR/BIS 51].

Householders named with household numbers
1801, 1811, 1821. **York**, par. St. Giles [YAO M14A and M15B:5].
1811. **York**, par. St. Cuthbert [BI PR/Y/CU 31] (at present not available, mislaid?); **York**, par. St. Martin, Coney Street [BI PR/Y/MCS 19]; **York**, par. St. Maurice [YAO K99].
1907. **York**, par. St. Cuthbert [BI PR/Y/CU 50-52].

Inhabitants
1723. List of 1,800 **York** inhabitants (with some relationships and occupations) who took oaths of allegience (under Act of 9 Geo. I) September to December 1723 [YAO City Council Minute Book F12 ff. 140-149].

YORKSHIRE, EAST RIDING

Abbreviations (see also page 12)
BI = Borthwick Institute, York.
HRO = Humberside Record Office, Beverley.
KHRO = Kingston upon Hull City Record Office.

Publications
The People of Hull in 1695 and 1697 (indexes to Hull censuses of 1695 and 1697), published (1990) by Kingston upon Hull City Record Office and East Yorkshire F.H.S. 92pp.

Note: Humberside Record Office, Beverley have compiled a collective surname index to some 17 local censuses at their office (see entries below), available in public search room.

All named with ages
n.d. **c.1871-80. Wetwang** (not a civil census) [HRO PE 48/67].

Yorkshire: East Riding *continued*

All named with births and marriages
1908-41. **Sutton upon Derwent** [BI PR/S/D 18].

All named
1695. **Kingston upon Hull** (all city wards except Humber ward) [KHRO CAT 92, 93, 95, 97-99], index published.
1697. **Kingston upon Hull** (all 7 city wards) [KHRO CAT 91, 94, 96], index published.
1834-44. **Bainton** (with children's ages or birthdates) [HRO PE5/42].

Householders named with household numbers
1801, 1811. **Lissett** [HRO PE 115/21, 22 with photocopies and indexes].
1801. **Hedon** [HRO DDHE 16/5 with index]; **Westow** [BI PR/WES 47].
1811, 1821. **Beeford** [HRO PE 114/118, 119 with photocopies and indexes].
1811, 1821, 1831. **Boynton** [HRO PE 143/22, 23, 24 with photocopies and indexes].
1811, 1821. **Dunnington** (chapelry in par. Beeford) [HRO PE 115/30, 31 with photocopies and indexes].
1811, 1821. **Hilston** [HRO PE 17/11 with photocopies and indexes].
1811, 1821. **Marfleet** [HRO PE 28/52 with photocopies and indexes].
1811. **Patrington** [HRO PE 38 acc.1484]; **Skipwith** (Skipwith township only) [BI PR/SKIP 15]; **Welton** [HRO PE 106/26 with photocopy and index].
1816. **Riccall** [BI PR/RIC 114].
1821. **Hedon** [HRO DDHE 16/88 with photocopy and index]; **West Heslerton** [BI PR/HESL/W 15].
1831. **Hedon** [HRO DDHE 16/16].
1838. **Etton** [HRO PE 52/44 with photocopy and index].
1918. **Norton** [BI PR/NORT 49].

Easter Books
n.d. **c.1450. Hornsea** [BI York Diocesan Records R.VII.F.102, 306].
1662?. **Sherburne in Hartford Lythe** [BI York Diocesan Records R.VII.H.2624].
1762-78. **Holme on Spalding Moor** [BI RE/H/SM 13].

Communicants Lists
n.d. **c.1680. North Cave** [HRO PE35/1].

YORKSHIRE, NORTH RIDING

Abbreviations (see also page 12)
BI = Borthwick Institute, York.
CAM = Cleveland County Archives Dept,
Middlesbrough.
NYRO = North Yorkshire Record Office,
Northallerton.

All named
1863-86. Aldborough [NYRO PR/ALB and
MIC 1854 frame 0487].

Householders named with household numbers
1811, 1821. Thirsk [NYRO PR/TH 6/10/18
and MIC 1627] (716 names in 1811; 743
names in 1821).
1811. Kilburn [NYRO PR/KLB/16 and MIC
1876 frame 3459]; **Middleton upon Leven**
[NYRO PR/MIL/6/5 and MIC 1204]; **South
Otterington** [NYRO PR/OTS/7/1 and MIC
1570 frame 1356].
1821. Huntingdon [BI PR/HUN 28];
Oswaldkirk [NYRO PR/OSW/8/1 and MIC
1856 frame 5700]; **Yarm** [CAM PR/YR/6/4].
1877. Leeming [NYRO PR/BED/22/12 and
MIC 2094].
n.d. c.1880. Bolton cum Redmire (Castle
Bolton only) [NYRO PR/BOC/9 and MIC
1259].

YORKSHIRE WEST RIDING

Abbreviations (see also page 12)
BDA = Bradford District Archives.
BI = Borthwick Institute, York.
CDA = Calderdale District Archives, Halifax.
DA = Doncaster Archives Dept.
DpL = Dewsbury Public Library.
HRO = Humberside Record Office, Beverley.
KDA = Kirklees District Archives, Huddersfield.
LDA = Leeds District Archives.
LCL = Leeds Central Library.
LUL = Leeds University Library.
NYRO = North Yorkshire Record Office,
Northallerton.
SA = Sheffield Archives.
WpL = Wakefield Library, Local Studies Dept.
WYA = West Yorkshire Archive Service HQ,
Wakefield.

Publications
*Householders named with household
numbers:*
1723. Wakefield [private collection] in
Wakefield Hist. Soc. Jnl., **5**, 58-73 (1978)
(1,431 names).
1780. Manningham (township in par.
Bradford) [original lost] in *History of
Manningham, Heaton and Allerton*, by W.
Cudworth (1896), 76-78, copy at CamGp.

All named with ages
1776. Wetherby [original in private
collection. Photocopies at LDA in Acc.
2679, and at WYA in Z90(L), and at LUL],
copy at CamGp.
1821. Ossett cum Gawthorpe (township in
par. Dewsbury) [WpL photocopy of original
in private collection].
1852. Swillington [LDA Par 63].

All named
1809. Tankersley and Wortley [SA Wh M 53].
1829. Warmsworth (some with ages) [LDA
BW/R/11 (box 27)], copy at CamGp.
1854-56. Selby (with years of birth) [BI PR/SEL
270].
1898. Swillington [LDA Par 64].
1922-23. Kirk Sandall [DA P13/4/F/1].

Householders named with household numbers
1723. Wakefield, see publications.
1764, 1811. Sowerby (township in par.
Halifax) [CDA STA:215/3 and SPL:166].
1780. Manningham, see publications.
1801, 1811. Elland cum Greetland (township
in par. Halifax) [CDA MISC:130].

Yorkshire West Riding: *Householders*
continued

1801, 1811. Hipperholme cum Brighouse
(township in par. Halifax) [CDA
MISC:7/115].
1801, 1811. Midgley (township in par.
Halifax) [CDA HAS:67], copies at CamGp,
copy of 1801 at SoG.
1801, 1821. Sandal Magna [WYA D20/327].
1801, 1821, 1831. Spofforth [LDA Par
118/17/1 and Par 131, 132].
1801, 1821, 1831. Swinton [DA P59/6/B/8/1,
2].
1801, 1811, 1821. Tong (township in par.
Birstall) [BDA Tong 12K/3, 6, 13].
1801. Bracewell [original at Lancashire R.O.
(not seen). Photocopy at LDA in Acc.2776];
Langfield (township in par. Halifax) [CDA
MISC:165/2]; **Leeds** (whole township except
north west and north east divisions) [LDA
LPC 104 with photocopies. Mf. copy at LCL]
(3,900 names); **Thrybergh** [SA PR106/4 pp.
14-15 and Mfiche copy].
n.d. clearly **1801. Newton Kyme** [BI PR/N/K
10].
1811, 1831. Snaith [HRO DDCL 200].
1811, 1821, 1831. Yeadon (township in par.
Guiseley) [LDA Aireborough UDC, Yeadon
Township Papers, and photocopy of 1811].
1811. Calverley [LDA Par 168]; **Carleton in
Craven** [LDA Par 149], copy at CamGp;
Farsley (township in par. Calverley) [LDA
'Pudsey B'; copies at LCL and Pudsey
Library]; **Honley** (township in par.
Almondbury) [KDA CP/Ho/Ce/1];
Todmorden and **Walsden** (township in par.
Halifax. Walsden wholly in Lancashire)
[CDA TT:185].

Householders continued

1821. Stansfield (township in par. Halifax)
[CDA TT:172]; **Thornhill** [DpL No.151
(misc. bundle)]; **Thurstonland** (township in
par. Kirkburton) [KDA KC 271]; **Warley**
(township in par. Halifax) [CDA OR:157/1;
photocopy at WYA in ZM4] (937).
1831. Hipperholme cum Brighouse (township
in par. Halifax) [CDA transcript of original in
unknown location in MISC:326/18]; **Nether
Hallam** (township in par. Sheffield) [SA CA
21(25)] (905).
1877. Skipton, par. Christ Church [NYRO
PR/SKP/12/4 and MIC 1899 frame 2588]

Easter Books
1572, 1574. Selby [BI Mf.(no ref)].
1596-1644, 1709-67, 1778-1801. Guiseley
(whole parish, also with Carlton, 1778+)
[LDA Guiseley Par 10, 20, 28, 31] also for
following townships in Guiseley par:
Rawdon, 1711-29, 1740-46 [LDA Guiseley
Par 14, 15, 18] and **Horsforth,** 1740-45
[LDA Guiseley Par 17].
1717-37, 1763-1812, 1814-29. Sandal Magna
[WYA D20/133-136].
1729. Thorne [BI York Diocesan Records
R.VII.I.955].
1737-39, 1763-70, 1780-1817. Wragby
[WYA D99/84-87, 91].
1750-93. Dewsbury [WYA D9/153, 154].
1751-60. Hemsworth [WYA D36/82].
1755-1801. Burghwallis [DA P54/2/B/1].
n.d. c.**1794. South Kirkby** [WYA
D168/3/2/21].
1795-1800. Wath and Mexborough [DA
P59/2/B/1/15]

Communicants Lists
1730-39. Cawthorne [WYA D148/3/2/1].

WALES

Abbreviations (see also page 12)
CaRO = Caernarfon Area Record Office (Gwynedd Archives Service).
DCRO = Dyfed Record Office, Carmarthen.
GmRO = Glamorgan Record Office, Cardiff.
GwRO = Gwent County Record Office, Cwmbran.
HCRO = Hawarden Branch, Clwyd Record Office.
NLW = National Library of Wales, Aberystwyth.
RCRO = Ruthin Branch, Clwyd Record Office.
RpL = Ruthin Public Library, Clwyd.
UCNW = University College of North Wales (Dept. of MSS.), Bangor.

ANGLESEY

Householders named with household numbers
1801. **Amlwch, Llannerchymedd** and **Llanwenllwyfo** [UCNW Bangor Mss. 1488].
1821. **Beaumaris** [UCNW Beaumaris and Anglesey Mss. 2/19-20].

BRECKNOCK or BRECONSHIRE

No relevant material has been located.

CAERNARVONSHIRE

Householders named with household numbers
n.d. c.1681 and 1686. **Llangystennin** [NLW SA/Misc/1417-8], copy at CamGp.
1794. **Caernarvon** [CaRO Ms. copy from original in private colln. XM/1395/306].
1815. **Aber** [CaRO X/pa ABER/133].

CARDIGANSHIRE

Householders named with household numbers
1821. **Llandygwydd** [NLW Par. Rec. no. 10].

CARMARTHENSHIRE

Householders named with household numbers
1821. **Llanarthney** [DCRO CPR/35/43].

DENBIGHSHIRE

All named with ages
1850. **Llansannan** [NLW par. rec. no. 4; photocopy at RCRO DD/DM/101/73].

All named
1864-76. **Cefn** [RCRO PD/17/1/10].

Householders named with household numbers
1681. **Chirk, Llanarmon Mynydd Mawr, Llanddulas, Llanrhaeadr ym Mochnant** and **Ruabon** [NLW SA/Misc/1307-1484], copies at RpL and CamGp.
1683. **Cerrigydrudion** [NLW SA/Misc/1307-1484], copies at RpL and CamGp.
1685. **Llanelian** [NLW SA/Misc/1307-1484], copies at RpL and CamGp.
1686. **Betws yn Rhos, Gwytherin, Llanddulas, Llandegla, Llanelian, Llanferres, Llangernyw, Llangollen, Llansantffraid Glan Conwy, St. George** and **Ysbyty Ifan** [NLW SA/Misc/1307-1484], copies at RpL and CamGp.
1687. **Llanfair Talhaiarn** [NLW SA/Misc/1307-1484], copies at RpL and CamGp.
n.d., 1680s. **Bryneglwys, Denbigh, Erbistock, Gresford, Gwytherin, Henllan, Llanarmon yn Ial, Llanddoget, Llandegla, Llandrillo yn Rhos, Llanelian, Llanfair Talhaiarn, Llanferres, Llanfihangel Glyn Myfyr, Llangadwaladr, Llangedwyn, Llangernyw, Llangollen, Llangwm, Llansantffraid Glan Conwy, Llansantffraid Glynceiriog, Llansannan, Llansilin, Llysfaen, Nantglyn** and **Ysbyty Ifan** [NLW SA/Misc/1307-1484], copies at RpL and CamGp.
1811. **Clocaenog** [RCRO PD/20/1/46].
1821. **Gresford** (Allington, Marford and Hoseley townships only) [RCRO PD/34/1/323]; **Henllan** [RCRO PD/38/1/315].

FLINTSHIRE

Householders named with household numbers
1681. Bodfari, Flint, Gwaenysgor, Halkyn, Hope, Llanasa, Newmarket (Trelawnyd) and **Ysceifiog** [NLW SA/Misc/1308-1486], copies at HCRO and CamGp.
1682. Caerwys [NLW SA/Misc/1308-1486], copies at HCRO and CamGp.
1684. Holywell and **Treuddyn,** par. **Mold** [NLW SA/Misc/1308-1486], copies at HCRO and CamGp.
1686. Cilcain, Cwm, Northop, Treuddyn, par **Mold** and **Ysceifiog** [NLW SA/Misc/1308-1486], copies at HCRO and CamGp.
n.d., 1680s. **Cilcain, Cwm, Dyserth, Halkyn, Holywell, Meliden, Nerquis, Northop, Rhuddlan, Tremeirchoin,** and **Whitford** [NLW SA/Misc/1308-1486], copies at HCRO and CamGp.
1811. Mold [HCRO D/KK/145] (1,026).
1816. Hawarden [HCRO D/BJ/347].
1821, 1831. Northop [HCRO P/45/1/201-2].
1831. Mold (Llwynegrin township only) [HCRO P/40/1/58].
1895-97. Meliden [HCRO P/39/1/42].
1901. Whitford [HCRO P/69/1/77].

Easter Books
1590. Mold [NLW Gwysaney Mss. no. 65].

GLAMORGAN

Householders named with household numbers
1921. St. Mary Church [GmRO P/23/CW/3].

MERIONETH

Householders named with household numbers
1681. Bettws Gwerfil Goch, Llandderfel, Llandrillo Edeirnion, Llangar, Llanymawddwy and **Mallwyd** [NLW SA/Misc/1305-1449], copies at CamGp.
n.d., c.1681. **Corwen** and **Llangower** [NLW SA/Misc/1305-1449], copies at CamGp.
1686. Llandrillo Edeirnion, Llangower and **Llangar** [NLW SA/Misc/1305-1449], copies at CamGp.
n.d., c.1686. **Bettws Gwerfil Goch** and **Corwen** [NLW SA/Misc/1305-1449], copies at CamGp.
n.d., 1680s. **Gwyddelwern, Llanfor** (2 lists), **Llansantffraid Glyndyfrydwy, Llanuwchllyn** and **Llanymawddwy** [NLW SA/Misc/1305-1449], copies at CamGp.

MONMOUTHSHIRE

Formerly administratively with England; now Gwent, in Wales.

All named
1699. Bassaleg [NLW Tredegar Mss and Documents no. 115].
1839, 1844, 1853. Machen [GwRO D.314.41-43] (temporarily withdrawn by incumbent of Machen).

Householders named with household numbers
n.d., c.1910. **Llanfihangel Crucorney** [GwRO D/Pa.6.55].

Easter Books
1752-61 Magor [NLW LL/Misc/436].

MONTGOMERYSHIRE

Householders named with household numbers
1681. Bettws Cedewain, Cemmais, Garthbeibio, Guilsfield, Llandysilio, Llanfechain, Llangadfan, Llanllugan, Llanllwchaiarn, and **Llanwrin** [NLW SA/Misc/1300-1490], copies at CamGp.
1682. Llanwyddelan [NLW SA/Misc/1300-1490], copy at CamGp.
·1684. Llandrinio [NLW SA/Misc/1300-1490], copy at CamGp.
1685. Garthbeibio, Llanerfyl, Llangadfan and **Welshpool** (as par. Poole). [NLW SA/Misc/1300-1490], copies at CamGp.
1686. Bettws Cedewain, Cemmais, Garthbeibio, Llanfechain, Llanllugan, Llanllwchaiarn, Llanmerewig, Llansantffraid ym Mechain, Llanwyddelan, Machynlleth, Meifod and **Newtown** [NLW SA/Misc/1300-1490], copies at CamGp.
n.d., 1680s. **Aberhafesp** (3 lists) **Berriew, Castell Caereinion, Darowen** (2 lists), **Guilsfield, Hirnant, Llandyssil, Llanerfyl, Llanfair Caereinion, Llanfyllin, Llanfihangel yng Ngwynfa, Llangynyw, Llangynog, Llanmerewig, Llanwddyn, Machynlleth, Manafon, 'Myvol Peniarth'** (Pennant?), **Newtown, Tregynon** and **Welshpool** (4 lists, 2 as par. Poole) [NLW SA/Misc/1300-1490], copies at CamGp.
1831. Penstrowed [NLW Par. Rec. no. 3].

PEMBROKESHIRE

No relevant material has been located.

RADNORSHIRE

No relevant material has been located.

ISLE OF MAN

Householders named with household numbers
1730. Douglas [Two versions have been
found: an 'official copy' of c.1800 in parish
register of St. Matthew, Douglas, at Manx
Museum Library, Kingswood Grove,
Douglas on Mfiche, and another copy
published in *Manx Society Jnl.*, **30** (3), 11-15
(1880). Copies of both at SoG and CamGp.
The published copy omits 37 households
given in the 'official copy' and varies from it
in some names and statistics given].

CHANNEL ISLANDS

JERSEY

Abbreviation:
SJ = La Societe Jersiaise, 9 Pier Road, St.
Helier.

All named
1788. St. Lawrence [SJ photocopy from lost
original in box file 33/20. Copy published in
Channel Islands F.H.S. Jnl., **8-14** (1980-82)].

Householders and men, 17-80, named with
ages and household numbers
1815. Jersey (whole island) [SJ copy from
original in Jersey Government Offices, on
shelf E8 in box file. Known as 'General
Don's Muster Roll'] (5,897 names).

Householders named with household numbers
1806. Jersey (whole island) [SJ copy from
original in Jersey Government Offices, on
shelf E8 in box file, with index to country
parishes. Copy at Channel Islands F.H.S.
Known as 'General Don's Muster Roll']
(4,363 names).

GUERNSEY

An 1821 census 'with names' for Vale is
believed to be held, amongst other parish
records, by: The Constables, Vale Douzaine
Room, Vale, Guernsey.

SCOTLAND

Abbreviations (see also page 12)
ACA = Aberdeen City Archives.
ApL = Annan Public Library, Reference Dept., Dumfries and Galloway.
AUA = Aberdeen University Library (King's College Special Collections Dept.).
AyA = Ayr sub-office of Strathclyde Regional Archives.
BCA = Blair Castle Archives, Blair Atholl, Perthshire (daily search fee – no postal searches).
CDL = Cunninghame District Library, Local History Dept., Ardrossan, Strathclyde.
CRA = Central Regional Archives, Stirling.
DDA = Dundee District Archive and Record Centre, Dundee.
DoA = Muniments of Duke of Argyll, Inveraray Castle, Strathclyde.
ELG = Elgin Library, Local Studies Colln., Grant Lodge, Elgin, Moray.
EUL = Edinburgh University Library, Special Collections Dept.
HRA = Highland Regional Archives, Inverness.
IpL = Inverbervie Public Library, Grampian.
MDA = Moray District Archives, Forres.
NES = North East Scotland Library Service, at H.Q. at Oldmeldrum, Aberdeenshire.
NLS = National Library of Scotland, Edinburgh.
NRH = New Register House, Edinburgh.
ODA = Orkney District Archives, Kirkwall.
OpL = Orkney Library, Kirkwall.
PCL = Paisley Central Library, Local History Dept., Strathclyde.
PDA = Perth and Kinross District Archives, Perth.
SHA = Shetland Archives, Lerwick.
ShL = Shetland Library, Lerwick.
SpL = Stonehaven Public Library, Grampian.
SRO = Scottish Record Office, Edinburgh.
SUL = St. Andrews University Library.
WCL = Wigtown County Library, Stranraer.

ABERDEENSHIRE

Publications
Householders named with household numbers: 1636. **Old Aberdeen** [ACA Council Register vol. 3, p. 3] in *Records of Old Aberdeen* , ed. A.M. Munro, **1**, 347-55 (Aberdeen, 1899), copy at CamGp. Also in *Scottish Notes and Queries*, **7** (1), 1-2, and **7** (2), 20-22 (June and July 1893).

All named
1789, 1791, 1794, 1797, 1801, 1804, 1812, 1815, 1825. Birse [SRO CH2/595/11-12. Mf. copies at NES, IpL and SpL]. Copies of 1789 and 1812 at CamGp.
1836, 1854-9. Forgue [SRO CH2/539/9].

Householders named with household numbers
1741. Meldrum and **Oldmeldrum** [AUA Duff of Meldrum Colln., M55 2778/10/18], copy at CamGp.
1801. Peterhead [NES] (826).

ANGUS (co. FORFAR).

Publications
All named: **1788. Craig** [SRO CH2/616/14] in *Craig, Angus, 1788 + 1791* by G. Johnson (Aberdeen and N.E. Scotland F.H.S., 1986).
Examination Roll: **1752. Arbroath** [Signal Tower Museum, Arbroath] in *Scottish Record Society*, new series, **13** (1987), ed. by F. Davidson.

Householders named with household numbers
1801. Dundee [DDA Town clerk's misc. no. 57, with index] (6,952).

co. ARGYLL

Publications
All named with ages/All named/Householders
named with household numbers (mixed).
1779. Duke of Argyll's Estate (large part of co.
Argyll, incl. Kintyre, Morven, Mull, Tiree
and Iona, also Roseneath, co. Dumbarton)
[DoA] in Scottish Record Society, **91** (1963),
ed. by E.R. Cregeen, copy at CamGp.

All named with ages
1792. Duke of Argyll's Estate (large part of co.
Argyll, incl. Kintyre, Morven, Mull, Tiree
and Iona, also Roseneath, co. Dumbarton)
[DoA in vol. with chamberlains accounts
and Kintyre feu duties, deed box: Rosneath
no. 8].

All named
1776. Island of Coll [SRO CH2/70/1].

Examination Rolls
1837. Kilfinan [NRH OPR 518/1].

co. AYR

All named with ages
1831. Kirkoswald [AyA CH2/562/27].

All named
1819/20. Stevenston [CDL MS60].

Householders named with household numbers
1821. St. Quivox [AyA CH2/319/22].
1822/4. Stevenston [CDL MS63].

co. BANFF

All named with ages
1841. Gamrie (draft civil census) [SRO
CH2/1051/3].

All named
1805, 1821. Mortlach [ELG bound vol. of
photocopies in L312.09411].
1820, 1826. Dufftown [ELG bound vol. of
photocopies in L312.09411].

Householders named with household numbers
1833-36. Ordiquhill [SRO CH2/291/7].

Householders named
1901. Glenrinnes (from civil census) [ELG
bound vol. of photocopies in L312.09411].

co. BERWICK

Householders named with household numbers
1811, 1831. Ladykirk [SRO CH2/660/4-5].

BUTE (Island of)

All named
1771, 1818, 1820. Rothesay [SRO
GD1/456/92, 192, 200].

CAITHNESS

No relevant material has been located.

co. CLACKMANNAN

No relevant material has been located.

co. CROMARTY

No relevant material has been located.

co. DUMBARTON

1779, 1792. Roseneath – see co. Argyll.

co. DUMFRIES

Publications
All named **1801, 1811, 1821.** Annan [ApL.
photocopy at SRO RH2/8/50] in *Scottish
Record Society*, new series, **4** (1975).

All named with ages
1791. Tundergarth [SRO CH2/831/1].

Householders named with household numbers
1840-41, 1842-43. Ruthwell [SRO
CH2/1155/12].

Examination Rolls
1697. Wamphray [SRO photocopy of old
transcript RH2/8/78].
1730. Gretna [held by Minister of Gretna].

co. FIFE

Householders named with household numbers
1821. Abdie [SUL CH2/828/10. Mf. copy at
SRO CH2/828/10].
1838. St. Andrews (Burgh of) [SUL B65/21/12].

co. INVERNESS

All named with ages
1765. islands of Rum, Eigg, Muck and Canna
[EUL David Laing Colln. La III.839] (1,157).

All named
1861-70, 1871-72. Invergarry (Glengarry and
Glenquoich estates only) [NLS MS 15164-5
and MS 15166].

Householders named with household numbers
1801. Lewiston (township in Glen Urquhart)
[SRO GD248/536/3].

co. KINCARDINE

All named with ages
1821. Dunnottar (old town of Stonehaven only) [SRO CH2/110/12. Mf. copies at NES, IpL and SpL].

All named
1798. St. Cyrus (old name: Ecclescraig) (giving ages of very old) [SRO CH2/590/1, pp. 27-42] (1,675).

Householders named with household numbers
1811, 1821. Dunnottar [SRO CH2/110/12. Mf. copies at NES, IpL and SpL].

Examination Rolls
1833, 1835, 1837. Dunnottar [SRO CH2/110/11. Mf. copies at NES, IpL and SpL].

co. KINROSS
No relevant material has been located.

co. KIRKCUDBRIGHT

All named
1684. Minnigaff, see co.Wigtown, publications.
1766. Lochrutton [SRO CH2/1344/16 and photocopy in RH2/8/64].
1841. Lochrutton (draft civil census) [SRO CH2/1344/21].

Householders named with household numbers
1821, 1831. Lochrutton [SRO CH2/1344/19-20 and photocopies in RH2/8/59].

Examination Rolls
1728-46, 1759-63, 1766-89. Lochrutton [SRO CH2/1344/1, 15-18 and transcripts in RH2/8/55-67].
1744-63. New Abbey [held by Minister of New Abbey].

co. LANARK

Publications
Householders named with household numbers: **1807. Cambuslang** (in some families all people named) in *A History of Cambuslang,* by J.A. Wilson (Glasgow 1929), copy at East Kilbride Central Library, Glasgow.

Examination Rolls
1783. Lesmahagow [NLS MS 8230].

EAST LOTHIAN
No relevant material has been located.

MIDLOTHIAN

All named
1780. Colinton [NLS Adv. MS 20.3.11].
1790. Edinburgh, par. St. Cuthbert [SRO CH2/718/211].
n.d., 18th century. Musselburgh [NLS MS 17868] (660).
1801. Stow [SRO GD113/465].
1834. Dalkeith (with children's ages) [SRO CH2/84/46-7] (5,500).
1835. Inveresk (whole parish except Inveresk village, Musselburgh and Fisherrow) [SRO CH2/531/59] (2,000).

Householders named with household numbers
1811, 1821. Dalkeith [SRO CH2/84/41-45].
1821, Glencorse [SRO CH2/181/22] copy at CamGp.
n.d., c.1830. Roslin [SRO CH2/181/22] copy at CamGp.
1831, 1833/37. Inveresk [SRO CH2/531/57-58].

Examination Rolls
1632-39. Edinburgh, par. West Kirk [SRO CH2/718/210].
1661, 1684, 1687, 1699. Edinburgh, par. Canongate [SRO CH2/122/67, 68, 98].
1687-90, 1741, 1744, 1749, 1755. Inveresk [SRO CH2/531/54, 55].
1699, 1700-03. Edinburgh, par. Duddingston and part par. **Canongate** [SRO CH2/125/1, 2].
1729-30. Edinburgh, par. St. Cuthbert [SRO CH2/718/211].
1743-51, 1757-63. South Leith [SRO CH2/716/327, 328].

WEST LOTHIAN

Examination Rolls
1660-70. Uphall [SRO CH2/362/1].
1683, 1692, 1694. Liberton [SRO CH2/383/3].

MORAY (co. ELGIN)

All named with ages.
1811. Dallas [MDA CH2/1129/2. Mf. copy at SRO CH2/1129/2] (871).

co. NAIRN

No relevant material has been located.

ORKNEY (Isles of)

All named with ages
1821. **Orphir** [ODA CH2/1093/16/13. Mf. copy at SRO CH2/1093/16/13], photocopy at OpL (906); **Deerness, St. Andrews, Sandwick, Stromness, South Ronaldsay, Burray, Swona** and **Pentland Skerries** (5 parishes) [private collection, but copies in search room at ODA] (7,653).

co. PEEBLES

No relevant material has been located.

PERTHSHIRE

All named with ages
1814. **Blair Drummond Moss** (appears to be whole par. Kincardine in Monteith) [SRO GD1/321] (1,500).
1820/21. **Moulin** [SRO CH2/488/20] (2,000).
1909. Duke of Atholl's Estates (mainly in par. Blair Atholl, Moulin, Logierait, Dunkeld, Dowally and Redgorton) [BCA].

All named
1791. **Aughtergaven** (Obney township only) [SRO GD121/box 42/224/1].
1806. **Moulin** [SRO CH2/488/19] (2,000).
1867, 1882. Duke of Atholl's Estates (mainly in par. Blair Atholl, Moulin, Logierait, Dunkeld, Dowally and Redgorton) [BCA].

Householders named with household numbers
1766. **Perth** (whole city) [PDA B59/24/1/36, with index] (1,792).
1811. **Longforgan** with **Invergowrie** [DDA P/Lo 4/1, with index].
1821, 1831. **Longforgan** [DDA P/Lo 4/6, 8].

Examination Rolls
1596-1611, 1660-67. **St. Madoes** [SRO CH2/1198/1].

co. RENFREW

Householders named with household numbers
1821. **Lochwinnoch** [PCL Cairn of Lochwinyoch (sic) Papers, vol. 18, p. 402].

co. ROSS

Householders named with household numbers
1792. **Barvas, Isle of Lewis** [Ness eccles. par. only) [SRO GD46/6/24].
1819. **Barvas and Uig, Isle of Lewis** (Uig gives numbers aged over 12 only) [SRO GD46/17/52, 53].
1825. **Gairloch** (Kernsary Estate only) [SRO GD46/13/156].

co. ROXBURGH

All named
n.d. c.1817. **Bowden** [SRO CH2/752/5].

Householders named with household numbers
n.d. c.1830. **Kelso** [SRO CH2/1173/172].
1831. **Jedburgh** [SRO CH2/552/44] (750); **Melrose**, with **Lindean**, par. Galashiels [SRO CH2/386/19] (728).

co. SELKIRK

Householders named with household numbers
n.d. c.1835. **Galashiels** [SRO GD237/16/5].

SHETLAND (Isles of)

Householders named with household numbers
1804. **Lerwick, Dunrossness, Yell, Sandsting** and **Aithsting, Bressay, Burra** and **Quarff, Nesting, Lunnasting, Whalsay** and **Skerries, Fetlar, Delting, Tingwall, Whiteness** and **Weisdale** (9 out of 13 pars. in Shetland) [SHA D11/179] (2,000). Copies at ShL and SoG.

co. STIRLING

All named
1793/4. Kippen [held by the Minister of Kippen].

Examination Rolls
1714-28, 1733-46. Buchanan [CRA CH2/606/10-13. Mf. copies at SRO CH2/606/10-13].
1789, 1791. Kippen [held by the Minister of Kippen].

co. SUTHERLAND

Householders named with household numbers
1811. Assynt, Farr and **Golspie** [HRA M/SUTH/12/5a, b, c].
n.d. clearly **1811. Reay** (part of par. in co. Sutherland only) [NRH OPR 40/1].

co. WIGTOWN (GALLOWAY)

Publications
All named with ages: **1832-34,** and *All named:* **1844-52. Portpatrick** [SRO GD1/335/2, 3] in *Scottish Record Society*, new series, **8** (1980);
All named aged over 12: **1684. Glasserton, Glenluce, Inch, Kirkcowan, Kirkcolm, Kirkinner, Kirkmaiden, Leswalt, Mochrum, Penninghame, Portpatrick, Sorbie, Stoneykirk, Stranraer, Whithorn** and **Wigtown,** with **Minnigaff, co. Kirkcudbright** (17 parishes). [SRO GD154/567 and photocopies in GD154/721 and RH2/1/79] in *Scottish Record Society*, **50** (1916), ed. by W. Scott.

All named
1791. Stranraer [WCL GWa31 (929.3)].

IRELAND

The following catalogue of pre-1901 Irish population listings has been compiled with the assistance of Rosemary ffolliott, Stephen Royle, Julian Walton and the Cambridge Group for the History of Population and Social Structure. Some other name lists are detailed in the three publications in 'Further reading' on page 10.

Abbreviations (see also page 12)
GO = Genealogical Office, Kildare Street, Dublin.
INA = Irish National Archives, The Four Courts, Dublin (formerly known as the Public Record Office of Ireland).
MDO = Meath Diocesan Office, Trim.
NLI = National Library of Ireland, Dublin.
PRO NI = Public Record Office of Northern Ireland, Belfast.
RCB = Representative Church Body Library, Dublin.

co. ANTRIM

All named with ages
1851. Aghagallon (townlands of Montiaghs, Tamnyrane and Tiscallen only), **Aghalee, Aghoghill** (townland of Craigs only), **Ballinderry, Ballymoney** (townland of Garryduff only), **Carncastle, Dunaghy, Grange of Killyglen, Killead** (townlands of Ardmore to Carnagliss only), **Kilwaughter, Larne, Rasharkin** (townlands of Killydonelly to Tehorny only), **Tickmacrevan** [INA. Mf. CEN 1851/2-13].

Householders named with household numbers
1766. Aghoghill [RCB]; **Ballintoy** [GO 536].
1820. Lisburn [PRO NI, T679/107-112].

co. ARMAGH

Publications
All named with ages: **1821. Derryhale**, (townland in par. Kilmore) [PRO NI, T 450] in *Ulster Folklife*, 7, 41-50 (1961).

All named with ages
1821. Kilmore [PRO NI, T 450] part published.

Householders named with household numbers
1766. Creggan [GO 537].
1770. Armagh City [Armagh Public Library, 9/5/20. Copy at PRO NI, T 1228/1].

co. CARLOW

No relevant material has been located.

co. CAVAN

Publications
All Church of Ireland people named: **1802. Enniskeen** [MDO] in *The Irish Ancestor*, 1973.

All named with ages
1821. Annagelliffe, Ballymachugh, Castlerahan, Castleterra, Crosserlough, Denn, Drumlumman, Drung, Kilbride, Kilmore, Kinawley, Larah, Lavey, Lurgan, Mullagh, Munterconnaught [INA Mf. CEN 1821/1-15].
1841. Killeshandra (except townlands of Corranea Glebe and Drumberry) [INA Mf. CEN 1841/1], copy: CamGp.

Protestant householders named with household numbers
1766. Kinawley, Lavey, Lurgan, Munterconnaught [RCB].

co. CLARE

No relevant material has been located.

co. CORK

Publications
Householders named with household
numbers: 1766. Dunbullogue, in *Jnl. Cork
Hist. and Arch. Soc.*, 51, 69-77 (1946); 1766
Kilmichael in *Jnl. Cork Hist. and Arch. Soc.*,
26, 69-73 (1920).
Protestants named: c.1830. Cork par. St. Mary
Shandon, in *Jnl. Cork Hist. and Arch. Soc.*,
49, 10-18 (1944).

All named with ages
1851. Kilcrumper (except townlands of
Glenwood, Lisnasallagh and Loughnakilly),
Kilworth, Leitrim (except townlands of
Ballymamudthogh, Cronahil and Propogue),
Macrony (townlands of Castle Cooke,
Kilclogh, Macrony and Shanaclure only)
[INA M4685].

All Protestants named
1834. Bandon (Ballymodan part only) [NLI
Ms.675].

Householders named with household numbers
1766. Aghabullog, Aghada, Ardagh and
Clonpriest (names wives and children),
Ballyhea, Ballyhooly and Killathy, Brigown,
Britway, Carrigdownane, Castlelyons,
Castlemartyr, Castletown Roche,
Churchtown, Clenor, Clondrohid,
Clondullane, Clonfert, Clonmeen, Ruskeen
and Kilcummy, Clonmult and Kilmahon,
Cloyne and Ballintemple, Coole, Farrihy,
Templemologga, Kildorrery, Nathlash and
Carrigdownane, Garrycloyne, Whitechurch
and Grenagh, Glanworth, Ightermurragh,
Imphrick, Inniscarra and Matehy,
Killogrohanbeg, Kilnamartyr, Kilshannig,
Kilworth and Macrony, Knockmourne and
Ballynoe, Lisgoold and Ballykeary, Litter,
Macroom, Magourney and Killcolman,
Mallow, Marshalstown, Midleton, Mourne
Abbey, Shandrum, Youghal [INA 1A 41 67];
Rathbarry and Ringrone [INA IA 46 49].

co. DONEGAL

Publications
Householders named with household
numbers: 1782. Culdaff, and
All Protestants: 1802-3. Culdaff (in 14 of 33
townlands) in *Three Hundred Years in
Inishowen* by A.I. Young (1929).

Householders named with household numbers
1766. Donoghmore [INA M207-8].

*Protestant Householders named with
household numbers*
1766. Leck [INA 1A 41 100].

co. DOWN

Householders named with household numbers
1766. Kilbroney and Seapatrick [RCB];
Shankill [INA 1A 46 100].

co. DUBLIN

All named with ages
1652. Baronies of Newcastle and Uppercross,
districts of Ballyfermot, Balliowen,
Ballidowde, Belgard, Bellemount,
Blundestown, Butterfield, Carranstown,
Crumlin, Dalkey, Deane Rath, Esker,
Feddenstown, Finstown, Gallanstown,
Great Katherins, Irishtown, Killnemanagh,
Killiney, Kilmainham, Kilmatalway,
Kilshock, Loughstown, Lucan, Milltown,
Nanger, Nealstown, Newcastle,
Newgrange, Newland, Oldbawn,
Palmerstown, Rathgar, Rathfarnham,
Rowlagh (Ranelagh), Rockstown, Shankill,
Symon, Tallaght, Templeogue, Terenure
(arranged by areas not parishes) [INA 1A 41
100].

Householders named with household numbers
1766. Crumlin and Donnybrook [RCB].
1831. Dublin, par. St. Bride [original in
Werburgh's Church, Dublin. Mf. copy in
NLI P1994, N2886].

*Heads of Families named in streets and
parishes*
1851. City of Dublin (22 parishes) [INA 1A 39
84-85. Mf. copies in CEN 1851/18/1-2. with
street index].

co. FERMANAGH

All named with ages
1821. Aghalurcher and **Derryvullen** [INA Mf.
CEN 1821/16-17].
1851. Drumkeeran (Clonee townland only)
[INA Mf. CEN 1851/13/1].

Householders named with household numbers
1766. Boho and **Derryvullen** [RCB];
Devenish, Kinawley and **Rossory** [GO 536].

co. GALWAY

All named with ages
1821. Aran and **Athenry** [INA Mf. CEN
1821/18-25], copy of Aran at CamGp.

All Church of Ireland people named
1827. Aughrim (with children's ages) [INA
M5359].

Householders named with household numbers
**1749. Ahascragh, Athleague, Ballynakill,
Drimatemple, Dunamon, Kilbegnet,
Kilcroan, Killian** and **Killosolan** [INA 1A 36
13].

co. KERRY

Publications
*Householders named with household
numbers:* **1834-5. Dunquin, Dunurlin,
Ferriter, Killemlagh, Kilmalkedar, Kilquane,
Marhin** and **Prior,** in *jnl. Kerry Arch. and
Hist. Soc.,* 7, 37-70 (1974) and 8, 114-135
(1975).

All named with ages
1821. Kilcummin [Royal Irish Academy,
Dublin: McSwiney Papers, Parcel F, no. 3].

co. KILDARE

All named
1840. Castledermot [NLI P3511].

co. KILKENNY

Publications
All named with ages: **1821. Aglish** and
Portnascully [GO 683-4] in *The Irish
Ancestor,* 8 (2), 113-124 (1976) and *The
Irish Genealogist,* 5 (3), 383-393 (1976);
Pollrone (incomplete) [GO 683-4] in *The
Irish Genealogist,* 5 (4), 522-6 (1977); **1841.
Aglish** (Aglish and Portnahully townlands
only) [GO 683-4] in *The Irish Ancestor,* 9
(1), 44-47 (1977); **1851. Aglish** par. with
Glengrant townland (in Portnascully par)
[GO 683-4] in *The Irish Ancestor,* 9 (2),
129-133 (1977).

All named with ages
1831. Aglish [GO 683-4].
1841. Rathkyran (Rathcurby and
Ballymountain townlands only) [GO 683-4].
1851. Portnascully (Clasharow townland only)
and **Rathkyran** (Ballincurra and
Ballymountain townlands only) [GO 683-4].

Householders named with household numbers
1766. Portnascully [GO Walsh Kelly
transcript].

KING'S Co. (OFFALY)

Publications
*Householders named with household
numbers:* **1766. Ballycommon** [GO 537] in
jnl. Kildare Arch. Soc., 7, 274-6 (1912-14).
All Church of Ireland members named: **1802.
Ballyboggan, Ballyboy, Castlejordan,
Clonmacnoise, Drumcullin, Eglish, Gallen,
Killoughey, Lynally, Rynagh** and **Tullamore**
[MDO] in *The Irish Ancestor* (1973).

All named with ages
**1821. Aghancon, Birr, Ettagh, Kilcolman,
Kinnitty, Letterluna, Roscomroe, Roscrea**
and **Seirkieran** [INA Mf. CEN 1821/26-34].
1835. Tubber [NLI P1994] (also see part of
par. in co. Westmeath).

Householders named with household numbers
1840. Eglish and **Drumcullin** [included in
Catholic parish registers of Eglish].

56

co. LEITRIM

All named with ages
1821. Carrigallen [transcripts from original in private collection at NLI P4646, N4658 and Leitrim County Library, Ballinamore].

co. LIMERICK

Publications
Protestant householders named with household numbers: 1766. Croagh, Kilscannel, Nantinan and Rathkeale, in *The Irish Ancestor* (1977).
Householders named with household numbers: 1834. Templebredin, in *jnl. North Munster Arch. and Hist. Soc.*, 17, 91-101 (1975) (also see part of par. in co. Tipperary)

Householders named with household numbers
1766. Abington, Cahircomey, Cahirelly, Carrigparson, Clonkeen, Kilkellane and Tuogh [INA 1A 46 49].

co. LONDONDERRY

All named with ages
1831-4. Aghadowey, Aghanloo, Agivey, Arboe, Artrea, Ballinderry, Balteagh, Banagher, Ballyaughran, Ballymoney, Ballynascreen, Ballyrashane, Ballyscullion, Ballywillin, Bovevagh, Clondermot, Coleraine, Cumber, Desertlyn, Derryloran, Desertmartin, Desertoghill, Drumachose, Dunboe, Dungiven, Errigal, Faughanvale, Kilcronaghan, Kildollagh, Killelagh, Killowen, Kilrea, Lissan, Macosquin, Maghera, Magherafelt, Tamlaght, Tamlaght Finlagan, Tamlaght O'Crilly, Tamlaghtard, Templemore and Termoneeny (compiled 1834 from 1831 census adding religious persuasions) [INA Mf. CEN 1831-4/1-44. Mf. copy at PRO NI]. Surname index at Research Centre, Derry Community Workshop, 10 Bishop Street, Londonderry BT48 6PW, N.I. and on Mfiche at SoG.

Protestants named
1847. Fallaghy [PRO NI D2098].

Householders named with household numbers
1766. Artrea, Desertlyn and Magherafelt [INA 1A 46 49]; Bovah, Comber, Drumacoose and Inch [INA 1A 41 100]; Desertmartin [RCB].

Protestant Householders named with household numbers
1766. Ballymascreen, Banagher, Dungiven and Leck [RCB].

co. LONGFORD

Protestants named
1731. Shrule [RCB].

Householders named with household numbers
1834. Granard [included in Catholic parish registers of Granard].

Protestant Householders named with household numbers
1766. Abbeylara and Russough [RCB].

co. LOUTH

Publications
Census: 1760. **Ardee**, in *The Irish Genealogist* (1961).
Householders named with household numbers: 1766. **Ardee** [INA 1A 41 100] in *jnl. of Co. Louth Arch. Soc.*, 10 (1), 72-76 (1941);
1766. **Creggan** [INA 1A 46 49] in *History of the Parish of Creggan* by Revd. L.P. Murray (Dundalk, 1940);
1834. **Tallanstown**, in *jnl. of Co. Louth Arch. Soc.*, 14 (1), 14-25 (1957);
'Military Census': 1798. **Drogheda**, in *jnl. of Co. Louth Arch. and Hist. Soc.*, 17 (2), 91-96 (1970).
Census: 1852. **Mosstown** (Mosstown townland only) and **Phillipstown** (Phillipstown townland only), in *jnl. of Co. Louth Arch. Soc.* (1975).

Householders named with household numbers
1766. **Ardee, Ballymakenny, Beaulieu, Carlingford, Charlestown, Clonkeehan, Darver, Drumiskan, Kildermock, Killeshiel, Louth, Mapestown, Phillipstown, Shanliss, Smarmore, Stickallen, Tallonstown** and **Termonfecken** [INA 1A 41 100]. Ardee published.
1766. **Creggan** [INA 1A 46 49], published.

co. MAYO

No relevant material has been located.

co. MEATH

Publications
All Church of Ireland members named:
1802-6. **Agher, Ardagh, Clonard, Clongill, Drumconrath, Duleek, Emlagh, Julianstown, Kells, Kentstown, Kilbeg, Kilmainhamwood, Kilskyre, Laracor, Moynalty, Navan, Robertstown, Raddenstown, Rathcore, Rathkenny, Rathmoylon, Ratoath, Skryne, Slane, Syddan, Tara** and **Trim** [MDO], in *The Irish Ancestor,* 5, 37-52 and 113-126 (1973).

All named with ages
1821. **Ardbraccan, Ardsallagh, Balrathboyne, Bective, Churchtown, Clonmacduff, Donaghmore, Donaghpatrick, Kilcooly, Liscartan, Martry, Moymet, Navan, Newtownclonbun, Rataine, Rathkenny, Trim, Trimblestown** and **Tullaghanogue** [INA Mf. CEN 1821/35-53].
1871. **Drumcondra** and **Loughbraclen** [transcript in Catholic parish registers].

Protestant Householders named with household numbers
1766. **Ardbraccan** [RCB].

co. MONAGHAN

No relevant material has been located.

QUEEN's Co. (LEIX)

No relevant material has been located

co. ROSCOMMON

Householders named with household numbers
1749. **Aughrim, Ardcarn, Athleague, Athlone,** par. St. John, **Athlone,** par. **St. Peter, Ballintober, Ballynakill, Baslick, Boyle, Bumlin, Cam, Clontuskert, Clooncraff, Cloonfinlough, Cloonygormican, Creive, Drimatemple, Dunamon, Dysart, Elphin, Estersnow, Fuerty, Kilbride, Kilbryan, Kilcolagh, Kilcooley, Kilcorkey, Kilgefin, Kilglass, Kilkeevin, Killinvoy, Killuken, Killumnod, Kilmacallan, Kilmacumsy, Kilmore, Kilnamagh, Kilronan, Kiltoom, Kiltrustan, Lissonuffy, Ogulla, Oran, Rahara, Roscommon, Shankill, Taghboy, Termonbarry, Tibohine, Tisrara** and **Tumna** [INA 1A 36 13].

co. SLIGO

Householders named with household numbers
1749. Aghanagh, Ahamlish, Ballynakill, Ballysumaghan, Drumcliff, Drumcolumb, Killadoon, Kilmacallan, Kilmactranny, Kilross, Shancough, Sligo and **Tawnagh** [INA 1A 36 13].

co. TYRONE

All Church of Ireland members named with ages
1851/2. Clogherny [PRO NI D10 4/32C/9/4/2 and 5 and T877 (839)].

Householders named with household numbers
1766. Aghalow, Artrea, Carnteel, Clonfeacle, Derryloran, Donaghendry, Errigalkerrouge, and **Kildress** [INA 1A 46 49]; **Drumglass, Dungannon** and **Tullynishan** [INA 1A 41 100].

co. TIPPERARY

Publications
Householders named with household numbers: **1834. Templebredin,** in *jnl. North Munster Arch. and Hist. Soc.,* **17,** 91-101 (1975) (also see part of par. in co. Limerick);
All Protestants named: **1864-70. Shanrahan** and **Tullagherton** [private collection] in the *Irish Ancestor,* **16** (2), 61-67 (1984); **1873, 1877, 1880. Clogheen,** in *The Irish Ancestor,* **17** (1), 25-30 (1985).

All named with ages
1799. Carrick-on-Suir [BL Add. Mss. 11,722. Mf. copy at NLI P28].
1821. Killinafe (East and West Curroghaneddy townlands only) [INA M242 and M346]

Householders named with household numbers
1766. Athassel, Ballintemple, Ballycahill, Ballygriffin, Boytonrath, Brickendown, Bruis, Cashel, par. St. John, Clerihan, Clonbeg, Cloneen, Clonoulty, Clonpet, Cloonbolloge, Colman, Cordangan, Corrogue, Cullen, Dangandargan, Drum, Dustrileague, Erry, Feathard, Gaile, Grean, Horeabbey, Killardry, Kilconnell, Kilfeacle, Killbrugh, Killea, Killevinogue, Killnerath, Kiltynan, Knockgrafton, Lattin, Magorban, Mealiffe, New Chapel, Pepperstown, Railstown, Rathcoole, Redcity, Relickmurry, St. Patrick's Rock, Shronell, Solloghodmore, Templebeg, Templemore, Templeneiry, Templenoe, Tipperary and **Toom** [INA 1A 46 49]; **Ballingarry** and **Uskeane** [GO 536].

co. WATERFORD

Publications
All named with ages: **1821. Ballygunner** (Callaghane townland only), in *Decies* (jnl. Old Waterford Soc.), **17,** 67-70 (1981).
1821. City of Waterford (incomplete), in *The Irish Genealogist,* **4** (1), 17-24 and **4** (2), 122-130 (1968).

Householders named with household numbers
1766. Killoteran [INA 1A 46 49].

co. WESTMEATH

Publications
All Church of Ireland members named:
1802-3. Ballyloughloe, Castletown Delvin, Clonarney, Drumraney, Enniscoffey, Kilbridepass, Kilcleagh, Killallon, Killough, Killua, Killucan, Leney, Moyliscar and **Rathconnell** [MDO] in *The Irish Ancestor* (1973).

All named with ages
1835. Tubber [NLI P1994] (also see part of par. in King's Co.).

59

co. WEXFORD

Publications
All Catholics named, most with ages: **1867.
Marshallstown** and **Kilmeashal** [NLI] in *The
Irish Genealogist*, 6, 652-669 (1980-5).

Householders named with household numbers
1766. Ballynaslaney [INA 1A 41 100].

*Protestant Householders named with
household numbers*
1766. Edermine [GO 537].

All Catholics named
1861. Enniscorthy [included in the Catholic
parish registers].

co. WICKLOW

*Protestant Householders named with
household numbers*
**1766. Ballymaslaney, Dunganstown,
Rathdrum,** and **Wicklow** [GO 537].